KU-486-097

GARDENING FOR PROFIT
From home plot to market garden
KATE COLLYNS

First published in 2013 by
UIT / Green Books
PO Box 145, Cambridge CB4 1GQ, UK
www.greenbooks.co.uk
+44 1223 302 041

Illustrations © 2013 Sarah Bartlett

Design by Jayne Jones

Front cover and page 3 image: Denis Tabler / Shutterstock.com

The inside cover photographs are by the author

ISBN: 9780857841308 (paperback)
ISBN: 9780857841353 (ePub)
ISBN: 9780857841360 (pdf)
ISBN: 9780857841377 (Kindle)

Printed by CPI Group (UK) Ltd, Croydon, CR0 4YY

Disclaimer: The advice herein is believed to be correct at the time
of printing, but the author and publisher accept no liability for
actions inspired by this book.

10 9 8 7 6 5 4 3 2 1

Contents

Acknowledgements

Thanks to all my family and friends, who went along with my strange second career choice. Thanks to Rowie Meers for her mentorship, and for allowing me to mess about in her tractors. Thanks to everyone at the Soil Association, especially Ben Raskin, and to many other generous and knowledgeable growers for their time and suggestions. Many thanks to the Prince's Trust, and to Richard Bowles and everyone at Hartley Farm for their continued support. Thank you Green Books for making this idea a reality, and to Sarah Bartlett for her gorgeous illustrations. Most of all, thank you James, for your constant belief and help.

To my father

Introduction

It's quite easy these days to find advice and guidance on growing food sustainably in your garden or allotment. But how does that translate to growing larger quantities in order to sell to your neighbours? And how about trying to make a living from doing this amazing and essential thing?

This guide is aimed at anyone who is interested in selling some produce for profit: whether surplus from a vegetable garden in the summer; or all year round from a fully developed professional local food business or community enterprise. It covers gardening for profit across the whole range of enterprise: so, while someone selling produce from an established home plot might not need advice on finding land, they will find the guidance on how to find a market, what to grow and how to sell produce very useful. At the other end of the spectrum, anyone planning a new market garden from scratch will be taken step-by-step through the intricacies of starting a business, and feel confident enough to get cracking.

I took the step from growing food for myself to growing on a larger scale a few years ago. I gave up my relatively secure office job to join the Soil Association's Apprenticeship Programme, part of the Future Growers Scheme, in 2008. Since then I've learned a huge amount about growing sustainably, and went on to start my own small business in 2010. However, it was very difficult to find advice from people who'd done the same thing: many growers I knew had started many years or even decades ago, or carried on the family business; plus they had a relatively large amount of land, selling produce to hundreds of people. Hard facts on smaller-scale growing, somewhere between large farms and gardens or allotments, seemed to be rare. Yet having a productive market garden is the dream of many, with the Future Growers Scheme annually oversubscribed, and hundreds of potential apprentices on the Soil Association's waiting list.

There is now a huge amount of interest in horticulture and agriculture – a real buzz around the industry – and a whole range of various apprenticeships and paths into farming and growing seem to appear every month.

When starting out, I muddled through as best I could, mining helpful and supportive fellow growers and farmers for information, and using the resources and funding at the Prince's Trust for young people wanting to start a business. I hope that this book will make the process much easier and give you the best start possible. All the resources mentioned throughout the book, together with many more useful contacts, are listed in the Resources section at the back.

Although it seems that there are lots of things to think about when setting up your own market gardening business, it's not as daunting as it might first appear. All the areas you'll need to address when starting up are broadly covered in these pages, and the advice should help you avoid any potential pitfalls. According to Lord Young's 2013 Report, micro businesses (those employing fewer than ten people) such as market gardens account for 95 per cent of all UK businesses, and are now gaining the recognition and attention that they deserve. Food production is, after all, one of the few really important career options – and the sooner food producers are valued as highly as some of the so-called 'wealth-makers' and celebrities in society, the better!

CHAPTER 1

The rewards of commercial growing

During and just after the Second World War, market gardens were the lifeblood of Europe: supply chains were short, food was fresh and healthy, and the local community came together to grow and eat food. That's not to glamorise these times, of course: market gardening involves lots of hard manual work, long hours and occasional despair when crops fail, pests descend and disease strikes. But despite these perils, producing food by hand on a small scale is rewarding – mentally, physically and spiritually. On a crisp frosty morning in January, or a balmy sunny day in July, even the downsides seem to make sense. Hard physical work keeps you fit and healthy (and you really feel like you've earned your dinner). Working outdoors raising and tending plants aligns you with the seasons: you probably won't mind working longer hours so much in the lighter summer days, and shorter hours in freezing winter. And it's a constant learning process – even (or especially) when crops fail, you are continually developing and deepening your understanding of and relationship with your garden.

Market gardens are perhaps the next logical step after running an allotment or large domestic garden: they operate on a relatively small scale, with the land area typically ranging from half to a few acres – of open fields, walled gardens, raised beds, greenhouses, polytunnels or a mixture of any of these. The difference between a garden and a market garden is of course the market: cash crops are sold in order to make the business viable. A wide variety of crops are crammed into these small spaces – and variety is, as they say, the spice of life. It's impossible to get bored when one minute you're sowing lettuce, the next picking spinach, then weeding sweetcorn, planting herbs or picking flowers for your eager customers – who all enjoy your produce almost as much as you do.

Eco-friendly growing

Since a common motivation for growing your own produce or growing food to sell on a small scale is so that you know exactly how that food has been produced, with artificial inputs such as pesticides, herbicides and fertilisers kept to a minimum, many small-scale holdings follow sustainable practices. 'Sustainable' growing means food production methods that can continue over a period of time without reliance on external inputs: for example by returning organic matter to the soil through compost, using green manures to feed the soil, keeping the soil ecosystem healthy through the use of crop rotations, and encouraging natural predators of pests. Being more self-sufficient in this way, such systems are therefore also more economical.

The terms 'organic' and 'sustainable' are often used interchangeably, but, while food that is certified as organic will have been produced with sustainable methods in mind, food described as 'sustainable' will not necessarily be certified as organic. The word 'organic' is a legally protected term when used to describe produce, but 'sustainable' growing in a market gardening context means systems that broadly follow organic standards.

The increased interest in sustainably produced food over the last decade may be for a wide variety of reasons. On the whole, studies have suggested that food produced to organic standards tends to contain a higher level of nutrients, as well as containing fewer harmful compounds and heavy metals, than 'conventional', chemically produced food. Apart from this most obvious benefit of local organic food – fresh and healthy produce, with real traceability – consumers also cite improving biodiversity, conserving water systems and the environment, and ethical and animal welfare factors as reasons to buy organic. Organic food production is also important with regard to cutting carbon emissions, since it uses no carbon-dependent fertilisers or pesticides; it also sequesters more carbon in the soil in the form of organic matter via composts, mulches and manures, which plants can reuse.

Industrial, huge-scale agriculture has of course become 'conventional' in the UK only relatively recently: surveys indicate that many members of the public still imagine farming and growing to involve the systems used 60 or more years ago, which are no longer called 'conventional' but are now described as 'sustainable', 'organic' or 'traditional' to show that they are different from the mainstream. While organically produced food can be more expensive than industrial chemically produced food, in the case of vegetables and fruit this is partly because of the difference in scale involved, as well as a result of the extra labour required for growing, weeding and harvesting in a sustainable system. Growing food is, after all, an incredibly labour-intensive manual job. But, as agriculture has increased in scale, we have lost touch with the basics, and prefer to use chemicals to fight pests, diseases and weeds from a distance rather than use our hands or mechanical tools (even though these usually do a better job in the long term).

However, with the depletion of cheaply available oil, the once-omnipresent nitrogen fertilisers and other agricultural chemicals have been steadily increasing in price (or have been banned because of environmental concerns), so it is hoped that 'conventional' producers will again see the merits of sustainable techniques, and that soon organic food will become more competitive in price. At the moment, cash-strapped consumers have to actively prioritise and really care about buying local, organic food (thereby helping not only themselves but also the local economy and the wider environment), since current supermarket-led prices encourage the consumption of ever-more-intensively farmed 'cheap' food, no matter what consequences to our health, animal welfare, our community or the environment. In a just world, the real costs of this type of food production – such as cleaning up waterways following run-off from fertilisers and pesticides, not to mention the extra burden on the NHS caused by nutrient-poor and calorie-rich foods – would be passed on to chemical farmers and food manufacturers rather than falling to taxpayers and charitable bodies.

Wider sustainability

Growing your own veg has undergone a real revival over the last few years, and allotment waiting lists are at an all-time high. Yet the next step, of selling surplus produce and starting a small business, seems out of reach for many people – if it occurs to them at all. But smallholdings, commercial allotments, market gardens and food-producing community projects are essential if we are to improve our local and national food security. Local food production also generates fewer carbon emissions from transporting produce around the country or further afield. More local producers means a healthy local economy too: in addition to the direct benefits of using local people (local knowledge, community building), there are myriad positive knock-on effects, such as cutting commuting times and therefore further reducing fossil fuel emissions, or encouraging other local food-based businesses to start up in order to take advantage of all the fresh produce around – perhaps leading to gastrotourism and the associated tourist-based advantages that would bring.

'Sustainability' does not just refer to the environment, of course, nor even to the local community: to be truly sustainable, a venture must be financially secure, or it cannot survive and inspire others. For example, there are a great many excellent charitable projects that incorporate food and growing as therapeutic activities, but unless these are securely funded in the long term, or can make enough money from other strands of the project such as selling produce, they cannot be viable. That is why this guide concentrates on the nitty gritty of setting up a food-producing business, running it, and staying afloat in the long term, with the aim of producing food in a local community for a living wage and fair return for all. This might not equate to a full-time income of course, if you have other commitments and would prefer to start a part-time micro business on a very small scale. But even tiny-scale businesses must be professional if they are to survive and be truly sustainable. For many, the aim of setting up a market garden is to provide a full-time income for themselves and perhaps for others too.

Professional growing

It should be said that well-meaning and competent hobbyists, who don't need to make a living from growing, can devalue food in a local area by selling off their surplus at a nominal price (or giving food away to those who would otherwise have bought local produce), thereby vastly undercutting professional growers who need the sales to survive. The risk is that if food is subsidised in this way for a period of time it prevents professional growers from making a living. And when the hobbyists have run out of produce, there will be nothing left from growers who have gone bust.

That's not to say that gardeners are irresponsible for giving away produce of course, particularly when it's to the needy, but it's worth keeping local professional growers in mind when doing so. On the whole, growers and farmers aren't trying to diddle anyone, or to charge more than their produce is worth: they are simply asking for a realistic living wage (often a much lower wage than is provided by other occupations) to enable them to continue producing great local food.

Points to consider before starting to grow commercially

If you are thinking of setting up a market garden, there are a number of factors to consider. The latter points in the list below are dealt with in detail in the following chapters, but the first five are more subjective – about you, the way you work and what you are able and willing to put into the project. It is worth spending a bit of time thinking about these before you go any further.

- Are you willing to put long hours (and possibly some of your own money) into setting up the business, and maintaining the garden?

- Will you be able to manage (financially and mentally) until the garden starts producing crops and making money?

- Can you cope with working on your own most of the time, or do you need people around you? Will you need extra help with all the weeding, planting and harvesting, especially in the busy summer time?

- What will happen if you're ill, injured or otherwise unable to garden?

- Will you choose to grow sustainably? If so, how will you manage weeds, pests and diseases?

- Where will the garden be?

- Will you need funding to set it up?

- What equipment will you need?

- Who will your customers be, and how will you get your produce to them?

- How will you market yourself?

- What's your long-term aim for your market garden?

CHAPTER 2

Finding land

Once you have decided that you would like to set up a market garden, probably the two most important questions to ask yourself are: Where will you grow your produce? And have you got someone to sell it to? You may know exactly what you want to grow, and who you would sell to, but have nowhere to do it yet. Or you may have some land you can use but are unsure how to go about selling, or what would be the most profitable crops to grow for various outlets. Finding appropriate potential customers is more complicated than finding land, since there are many factors to consider – price, presentation, demographic, competition and so on – so good market research is critical. It's important to have both your land and potential market firmly in mind before going any further.

The next chapter is all about finding a market to sell your produce to. This chapter deals with how to go about getting land. If you already have a large enough plot, or an allotment that does allow commercial growing, you can skip to the next chapter now.

If you don't already have a piece of land, it can be difficult to know where to start looking for something suitable. There is a range of options available for those who are not in a position to buy: from straightforward tenancies to Land Trust and CSA schemes, or community projects with land attached. Which option is right for your business will depend on the individuals involved, and on the kind of garden you want to start.

Once you've identified a piece of land that seems suitable, it's a good idea to send off a soil sample to an accredited laboratory to find out more about its pH, structure, mineral and nutrient levels.

Buying land

Your dream may be to buy your own little piece of heaven: if you do have the money, you can try asking local estate or land agents whether they have any agricultural land on their books that falls into your preferred size and price range. The Agricultural Land

Classification system in England and Wales is part of the planning system, and classes farmland into six grades (seven in Scotland). Grades 1, 2 and 3a are classed as 'Best and Most Versatile Land' (Excellent Quality, Very Good Quality and Good Quality respectively), and are protected from development. Ideally you'd want these for horticulture, since Grades 3b, 4 and 5 (Moderate, Poor and Very Poor Quality) are recommended only for cereals (Grade 3b) or permanent pasture (Grades 4 and 5). Scotland uses the similar Macaulay Land Capability for Agriculture (LCA) classification – the thirteen classes and divisions of the system are broadly simplified into four categories of land: Arable Agriculture (LCA classes 1-3.1), Mixed Agriculture (LCA classes 3.2-4.2), Improved Grassland (LCA class 5.1-5.3) and Rough Grazing (LCA classes 6.1-7). In both systems, the lower the grade number, the better-quality the land. However, I know growers who eventually managed to restore structure and fertility to very poor land – which is also usually cheaper to buy of course – but if you take this route, expect lots of hard work and yields to be poor for years.

Some old brownfield sites might seem perfect for a market garden, and these may also be near towns or even in cities, so ideally located for serving customers. However, be aware that old industrial sites that look nice and verdant may be masking toxic land underneath: many industries such as mining, smelting, gasworks and so on can result in contaminated land. In these instances, it's worth including a test for toxins as part of your laboratory soil analysis.

The main stumbling block when looking for small pieces of land suitable for market gardens is that they are often snapped up as pony paddocks: demand is high, which pushes the price up further. Generally, the more land you can buy, the cheaper the price per acre (market gardens still seem to be measured in acres rather than hectares on the whole, probably because it makes them sound larger!). For smaller plots – up to an acre or so – the price is extremely high: on average you'll be lucky to find something suitable for less than £12,000/acre in the south of England; compared to the overall agricultural land average of just over £7,400 per acre.* As the old adage goes: 'Buy land – they don't make it any more.' This is especially true on an island nation such as Britain, where demand for land is always high, and investors gamble on being able eventually to gain planning permission for development and housing. Owning land is therefore out of reach for many of us.

Land Trust and share farming

Access to land has been an increasingly hot topic over recent years: a number of worldwide organisations are campaigning for better access to land for those who want it; one example being the International Peasant's Movement Via Campesina, which promotes small-scale farming and strongly opposes corporate-driven agriculture. One positive measure that a group of organisations has made is to set up the Land Trust

---

* Royal Institution of Chartered Surveyors (RICS), August 2013.

(known as the Soil Association Land Trust, it is administered by the Soil Association but with its own board of trustees). Landowners and farmers can donate some land to the Trust, or leave a whole farm to it in their wills; the trustees then ensure that tenants using the land adhere to organic principles and manage the land in the way the donors would wish. In this way, landowners are assured that their life's work will carry on, and they get to give landless farmers and growers a chance to farm and grow food.

Some of the Land Trust programmes already up and running are examples of share farming, whereby a landowner and a tenant both run their businesses on the same land. This works especially well when the businesses have a slightly different focus: so, for example, you could try approaching a local chicken or sheep farmer and suggest including a few acres of field-scale vegetables in their rotation, which you would run as a business; you may also be able to negotiate establishing some structures such as polytunnels or semi-permanent perennial beds, permanent plantings such as an orchard and so on. Agroforestry (integrated farming combining trees or shrubs with crops or livestock) is really coming into its own now: many farmers are realising the benefits of having a second income stream and at the same time providing shelter for their huge fields of

cereals or livestock, making them more productive; not to mention the biodiversity benefits. You might therefore find many farmers receptive to the idea of growing a mixture of crops in strips around the farm.

The Ecological Land Co-operative (ELC) is a social enterprise and co-operative established to provide affordable sites for ecological land-based livelihoods. They can provide opportunities for new organic entrants to set up their own smallholdings. It's worth finding out what's currently available via their website, or contact them directly to ask whether any opportunities are about to come up.

Once you've found somewhere suitable for a share farming project, you then negotiate a rent or share of the business's turnover or profits. Another benefit of running a horticultural enterprise alongside an agricultural business is that you can swap some of your waste veg, weeds and pests (such as caterpillars and slugs) for manure or other useful by-products, which also helps to keep costs down for both parties.

Share farming doesn't have to be on a large scale of course. I know of several arrangements where part-time gardeners grow their produce on a neighbour's land or large garden – the landowner gets the benefit of that space being looked after and managed, and also gets a small amount of the produce every now and then.

Tenant farming

Two of the largest landowners in the UK are the National Trust and the Church of England. The National Trust owns 255,000ha (630,000 acres) of land, and has a vast range of farms, walled gardens and holdings. Up to 60 per cent of its land is rented out to farmers and growers on varying contracts, and it is worth approaching the organisation to see if there is anything suitable in your area. Many National Trust properties and country houses are also keen to add local food production to their brand, and can offer a farmers' market, café or shop as an outlet (not to mention their staff and vast army of volunteers as potential regular customers).

The Church owns over 48,000ha (120,000 acres) of land in rural areas alone, and is also landlord to a large number of tenant farmers. Ask your local minister or verger whether your church owns some local land that might be suitable, or who best to contact to find out about land further afield. Some large organisations such as the Church tend not to have much detailed information available in a centralised office, so you are better off trying to approach local representatives if possible.

Parish councils also own a quantity of farm and land plots, aside from allotments; however, contracts tend to be long term (and often come with houses and lots of land), so vacancies don't come up very often. Keep an eye on their websites, and contact your local authority directly to ask if they have anything suitable.

Private farms or country houses are also a fertile source of possibilities. Those with farm shops or existing direct sales outlets are likely to be especially interested in your idea: farm shops have to have a minimum of 70 per cent local produce in order to describe themselves as such, and having a vegetable-growing business actually on the site will be an extra draw to the shop. This kind of situation is ideal: you have a ready-made outlet waiting for you, plus farmers with farm shops are usually very happy to help you get started and will have useful equipment available. There are often endless other benefits for both parties: if you can sell excess produce elsewhere, that's another advert for your plot of land and the farm shop too – and the farm shop will be keen to promote your products because they're as local as possible, and reinforce the idea that the farm shop sells produce grown right there on that land. Try organisations such as the Organic Growers Alliance (OGA), the National Farmers' Union (NFU) or World Wide Opportunities on Organic Farms (WWOOF) for a list of farms in your area; or simply ask at your local farm shop.

Many old country houses have walled gardens, which may be available for a market garden project, so check out your local private grand houses and estates. Some may have fallen into disrepair and been neglected for years, so even if you're able to find out who owns them, and your business idea is welcomed, be prepared for a lot of work. Old walled gardens may have disease problems such as onion white rot too, so see if you can find out the history of the garden, and what it typically used to grow, to prevent heartache later when crops might fail. Soil tests are definitely advisable. On the other hand, country houses could be an excellent ready-made market to sell to, and you'll have a prestigious and respected address that will be easy to find.

Corporate ladder

Farms and estates are not the only businesses with land, of course. Many companies (especially larger corporations) either own or rent plots of land or garden spaces that seem pretty incongruous to the business, and may not even be near the main premises. A large number of corporations also have dedicated teams for community and environmental projects, and run volunteer days for their staff to work on charity projects or conservation work. You could pitch a sustainable market garden to them, with the suggestion that staff sign up to come and help out perhaps one day a month (if it's a large staff, that's a lot of valuable help!).

Your volunteers get to learn about growing, soil, biodiversity and food production, as well as enjoying some time out of the office, and the company gets to tick the boxes that say Corporate Responsibility, Employee Well-being and Environmental Scheme (there are also various corporate awards for companies that make a positive difference to their surroundings). And of course you get some land and a workforce – and perhaps a market to sell to, with discounts and special offers for volunteers. Having a detailed and professional business idea or plan is of course important when approaching any prospective landlord, but this is especially true when approaching businesses.

Community projects

The previous suggestions have been from the perspective of a grower trying to find land and a market – but there may already be some projects in place that have land but no grower. Community Supported Agriculture (CSA) schemes have been developing steadily in the UK over the last five years: although the schemes vary enormously, they are all partnerships between farmers or growers and the local community, providing mutual benefits and reconnecting people to the land. In many cases this means that a community group has got together and expressed a desire for good, local food, so they employ a professional grower (or growers), and get local people to register for the CSA, paying money up-front for the year's produce. If the harvest is poor that year, the farmer/grower has shared the loss with the CSA members rather than taking all of the hit; likewise, if it's a bumper crop, everyone will benefit and enjoy the abundant produce.

Many innovative schemes also include work days, where members come and work in exchange for produce – this is fantastic when it comes to weeding and harvest times (although, as with any volunteer programme, this should not be relied upon but rather seen as a bonus).

This model offers many benefits to growers; not least security. Some projects will also have most necessities in place, such as land arrangements, and be able to raise funds to get any other equipment you might need. However, there is less autonomy than starting up your own business: depending on the set-up, you might need to make most decisions by committee, such as what to grow, whether to sell any surplus elsewhere, where to source equipment such as a polytunnel, whether to employ another grower and so on.

This kind of community project often overlaps with the Transition Network. The Transition movement started in order to prepare communities for a future without relying on oil; now it's grown into a huge, global initiative that supports community-led responses to climate change and shrinking supplies of cheap energy, building local resilience and well-being. A large number of towns and cities all over the UK already have a Transition movement, and many of the same people are involved in other community food projects such as CSAs. It's worth finding out if there is a Transition group already in your area – they may well be looking for growers to start small local businesses or to kick-start their community project.

Finding land checklist

- If you want to buy, think about whether you would do so alone, or in partnership with other people, and whether you would need to borrow money.

- If you are thinking of renting, consider all kinds of landowners, including less obvious future holdings, such as 'gardens' belonging to corporations, or any land already held in trust for local environmental movements.

- Think about whether share farming might suit your market garden idea: consider the benefits other businesses based on the same land could bring you, and the benefits that you could offer others.

- Consider the community element: if you would like to involve your local community in your garden, to what extent? If you are thinking of Community Supported Agriculture, would you prefer to just have a grower's job or to have more control over the project?

- When you've identified some suitable land, check its history and get a soil analysis.

CHAPTER 3

Finding a market

Market research is an essential part of setting up your business. You may have found the perfect piece of land to grow on, but if it's miles from the nearest town or village, and your transport, storage and packing facilities are limited, it could turn out to be a poor choice. There is a huge range of options when it comes to finding a market to sell to: some routes are tried-and-tested, while others will need more energy and creativity to get the sales – but might prove more fruit-ful. Finding a variety of outlets is important, because you won't then be dependent on one revenue stream.

Potential outlets

A good start in your market research is to draw up a list of possible outlets, including some from the ideas outlined in this section, then approach each one to see how much interest there is in local, sustainable, fresh food in the area. Explore the local area well to sniff out these places – in person, via word of mouth, online or just using a phone book.

Farm shops, garden centres and health shops

Farm shops are probably the most obvious outlet for local produce. The term 'farm shop' also now seems to encompass artisan producers, cider makers and delicatessens, rather than just the old-fashioned end-of-a-barn efforts (although these too are very popular). Independent garden centres are also good places to consider, for selling both your grown produce and also any excess potted young plants or herbs for other gardeners to grow on.

Wholefood and health shops are always on the lookout for healthy local produce, to give them the edge over larger high-street chains. Don't forget that retailers are eager for something that their customers can't find anywhere else, and which makes the shop memorable. If your land is close to or within a town or city, shops such as these are a very promising source of customers. It's not just specialist food shops either – a local village shop and post office will often gladly take locally produced vegetables; this feeds into the community spirit of these establishments, and helps them compete with larger supermarkets and chains.

Restaurants and catering

Catering industry outlets are also a great market to try: even if the nearest community is a tiny village, there is sure to be a local pub nearby who could use your lovely fresh produce. Cafés and tea shops are also often receptive, especially the more boutique cafés, who actively source good ingredients. As a rule, the smaller and more independent restaurants will generally be more willing to take produce in smaller quantities from a local grower; as with bigger shops, large chain restaurants will most likely have contracts with bigger wholesalers and may not place so much emphasis on local food.

Many caterers also like to use local producers where possible for their events: try community noticeboards, local magazines or online to find their details. If you're in a location that hosts festivals, ask the organisers for a list of food stallholders so you can approach them and find out what kind of produce they're looking for, and the quantities needed.

You could also contact event venues such as private woodlands or country houses directly; stately homes are often used for weddings and other events, so may be interested.

Veg box schemes

If you have enough land to grow a good range of crops throughout the year, then setting up a veg box scheme for your local area might be a viable option. Depending on your location and transport, you could offer home delivery, or drop boxes or bags of vegetables and fruit off to collection points (shops, pubs, offices, community centres, surgeries, schools . . .). This option could be well suited to a community that doesn't have much in the ways of local shops and facilities, and would otherwise find it difficult to find local food.

You wouldn't necessarily have to run the scheme all year; some offer boxes only between June and February, for instance, and stop over the 'hungry gap' from March to May, when very little is available. Larger box schemes buy in produce to fill this gap, and cover any crop failures. Setting up a box scheme does involve a lot of administration, however, so may be something to work up to, or you could think about starting off on a small scale, with perhaps 10-20 local customers, and see how it goes.

Market stalls

There are now around 750 farmers' markets across the UK, plus many more general street markets selling a wide variety of products, including food. Waiting lists for more established farmers' markets can be very long, but it's worth a try. Consider sharing a market stall with another producer to cut costs and ensure regular supply. There are always artisan markets starting up, so keep your eyes and ears open for new outlets – or simply set up your own market on a likely street corner or square (contact your local council for permission). If there are already several veg producers in the market you have in mind, you probably won't sell a huge amount unless you offer something a bit different – such as specialising in unusual salad leaves all year round, or edible flowers, for instance.

Some farmers' markets are rather infrequent, and many customers won't be able to wait more than a week to buy their next supply of fresh produce, so if your market is not weekly, don't expect to sell a weekly-shop's-worth of veg to people. Most likely you'll sell only a few items at a time to most customers, or produce that is unavailable elsewhere, unless you can build up a dedicated following (see Chapter 10 for ideas on how to maintain customer loyalty).

Pick your own

Pick your own (PYO) schemes have fallen out of favour of late, probably at least in part due to perceived health and safety restrictions, as well as poor returns. Many health and safety regulations are simply common sense, and some worries may be unfounded, but the idea can still seem like too much hassle in today's 'claim culture'. However, variations on the PYO theme can be a great way of getting your community involved: customers see exactly how their food

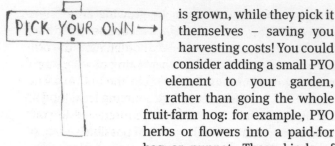

is grown, while they pick it themselves – saving you harvesting costs! You could consider adding a small PYO element to your garden, rather than going the whole fruit-farm hog: for example, PYO herbs or flowers into a paid-for bag or punnet. These kinds of crops also have the added advantage of being less appealing to eat on the spot!

If you'd rather stay in control of the picking (and con-suming), it's possible to compromise and take orders from customers when they arrive, then go and pick for them while they wait. This kind of scheme is probably best suited to locations near main thoroughfares or close to towns, and may depend on seasonal tourists and visitors, which in turn is likely to depend on the weather. Picking each order individually is also very time-consuming and not terribly efficient; an alterna-tive might be for customers to order ahead, a bit like a bespoke veg box scheme, then you can pick what you need that day in one go. Customers may also be will-ing to pay extra for the bespoke service.

The public sector

Schools, hospitals and council offices can also be good outlets to consider – but they will tend to require bulk quantities of staples such as potatoes, carrots and cabbage, rather than the more expensive and unusual salady items. If you're growing on a larger scale, however, then a public procurement contract can mean a nice solid and regular order. After the processed meat scandals at the beginning of 2013, many more schools are now keen to join the Soil Association's Food for Life Partnership, sourcing local food as much as possible, so may well be interested in your produce. Primary schools too are a possible source of more feasible contracts, since they are usually smaller than secondary schools, and there is often a greater enthusiasm for and flexibility about including food and environment topics in classes for younger children. Some schools also hold market stalls to sell local produce, or even produce that they've grown themselves (this could be a good partnership, if you can spare some of your land for them to grow on, or time to give them a hand on theirs).

Even if you don't grow enough of a crop to supply the bulk needed by a hospital or nursing home, for example, it might also be worth approaching such institutions to see if they'd consider taking fresh local produce for any visitors' cafés or kitchens, which would require smaller batches of vegetables and herbs.

Consider the competition

Finding potential places and customers to sell your produce to is only one part of market research. While researching the demand for fresh local produce in your area, you'll probably come across a number of businesses who may be potential competitors. While the existence of such trade does indicate that there is demand for fresh produce, of course that demand is being at least partly met already by those businesses. You'll need to think about what you could offer customers in order that they choose your produce instead (or as well as) your rivals': will it be fresher? More sustainable? Better value? (Value and price can be a slippery slope, though, and price wars are best avoided for smaller producers.) Will you be the only business in the area selling a particular crop? More convenient? Friendlier and more reliable? Will you offer a wider range of vegetables? Finding your own unique selling point (USP) is essential when you come to market your produce.

You'll need to have a good idea of exactly who and where your competitors are, and what their individual strengths and weaknesses are. For example, a larger wholesale business will have the advantage of relatively low-priced crops, larger quantities and a wide range of produce available – but crops will not usually be so fresh, since many wholesalers store produce between collecting from growers and delivering to customers. Furthermore, the business may be rather inflexible when it comes to last-minute order changes, and there may be a minimum order.

Don't overlook the possibility of turning potential rivals into new outlets and opportunities: you will most likely be aiming at slightly different markets, but you could always sell some produce wholesale to existing box schemes and market stalls, for when they start running short. When starting your market research and talking to existing producers, ask them whether they'd be interested in such a deal, and perhaps what they would be interested in buying in to supplement their own produce.

A common market research phrase is 'SWOT analysis', which stands for: strengths of, weaknesses of, opportunities for and threats to your proposed business. This is a useful tool for assessing the context of your business.

- Your USP(s) will be a strength, as will things such as the environmental sustainability of your system in an uncertain future: who knows what the weather will be like next year (or even tomorrow), or whether the public will care about sustainable fresh food? (See Chapter 10 for more on future challenges.)
- Think hard about what your weaknesses are, or could be: you don't necessarily have to change your plans because of them, but just be aware that they exist, and act to lessen their impact as much as possible. For example, being small scale will probably mean that your prices will be higher than those of larger wholesalers. Rather than dropping your prices, a way to address this could be to market the 'local, sustainable and fresh' angle, so that customers understand what they are paying for. It might be worth concentrating on higher-value crops, such as leafy veg, rather than cheaper stored staples such as potatoes, for example, to really demonstrate the difference.

- An opportunity for your business could be, for example, that a local chef has posted an advert asking for local produce: think about how you could exploit and build on this interest.
- An example of a threat might be that your customers enjoy your produce so much that they decide to grow it themselves! One way to act on this would be to concentrate on crops that require skill and special equipment such as polytunnels; or you could sell young plants to these enthusiastic gardeners.

Detailed research

It's a good idea to research some concrete facts and figures, especially when you come to drawing up a business plan (see Chapter 5). National or local surveys on food trends, news stories, the latest statistics on peak oil and industry market figures are all useful when building up a picture of how your business will work. This desk research is perfect for explaining your reasons for starting a business to any prospective funders or supporters, and should be backed up with any relevant experience you might have growing and selling food in your area. This 'field research' could include the impressions you got when looking after a market stall for a friend, or the vegetable sales and turnover figures from a local shop, if you can get them.

Test-trading is a great way of getting feedback and working out how your garden will run, and what will sell: even if you can only sell a few herb bags from some pots on your windowsill for now, you will get a feel for how customers will react to your produce, and what they will be willing to pay.

Meeting and talking to people is perhaps the best way to gauge likely interest – but if you're approaching shops or third-party outlets, they may be unsure as to the demand for your planned produce, if it's something they haven't tried before.

Another good strategy is to put together a simple questionnaire and leave it in shops, doctors' receptions or pubs, for example (depending on the outlets you plan to sell to), for prospective customers to fill in. It's also a good way to introduce yourself and your plans to the community, and to start building a potential customer base before you even start growing. You can make a questionnaire as detailed as you like: perhaps asking whether people would be interested in locally produced sustainable food; if so, where or how they'd like to buy it; what in particular they'd be keen on; and also whether they'd be interested in getting involved themselves, for example by volunteering. Bear in mind, though, that the more information you ask of people, the less likely they are to fill the questionnaire in! It should be easy and quick to read and answer.

Overleaf is the questionnaire I put together before starting my market garden: I left a stack of these for about a month (with some pens!) in the farm shop and café where I rent my land, and got about 40 written responses plus a few verbal suggestions, which were

Fruit & Veg Questionnaire

Hello! My name is Kate Collyns, and I'm about to start growing fruit, vegetables and herbs using sustainable methods here at Hartley Farm, available to buy soon through the farm shop. I'd really love to know what kinds of vegetables *you* want, and would appreciate your thoughts if you could spare one minute to answer this quick questionnaire

1. Which of the following are important to you when choosing your fruit and vegetables? Please rate the below from 1, least important, up to 5, most important
Cost
Organic/sustainably grown
Locally grown
Appearance/size
In-season produce

2. Would you be more likely to buy certain vegetables, herbs and fruit if there was a recipe handy to give you ideas on what to do with them? Please circle one of the below, and state the produce that needs ideas
No difference
More likely
Definitely

3. Would you like to get more involved in how your food is produced, such as volunteering for a few hours a week, or applying for an allotment at the farm? If so, please leave your name and email addresss or phone number overleaf
No
Yes, I'm especially interested in:

>>

4. Which of the following more unusual items, if any, would you like to see on sale, homegrown here on the farm? Please circle all that apply

 Globe artichokes

 Fennel

 Chilli peppers

 Salsify

 Mixed herb bunches

 Flower salads

 Mixed salad leaf bags

 Sprouting seeds

 Mini cucumbers

 Celeriac

 Coloured cauliflowers

 Curly kale

 Red Russian kale

 Cavolo nero kale (black lace/Tuscan kale)

 Turnips

 Raspberries

 Blueberries

 Gooseberries

 Blackcurrants

 Whitecurrants

 Redcurrants

Herb pots – particularly...

Anything else...

5. Are there any other comments, thoughts, dislikes or suggestions about vegetables, fruit and herbs that you'd like share? Any favourite veggies?

Thank you for your time; please leave your filled-in questionnaire at the till in the farm shop.

 **hartley**Farm

very interesting and helpful. It's worth keeping in mind the fact that while respondents might say that price isn't the most important factor when buying vegetables, sometimes cost might well be the decider when shopping on a budget – so take your questionnaire results with a pinch of salt.

Finding a market checklist

- Find your potential customers (e.g. shops, restaurants, events venues, direct sales), and approach them to learn about what they want.
- Work out your unique selling points (USPs).
- Compare your business's strengths and weaknesses to those of your competitors.
- Research concrete facts and figures as part of your analysis.
- Find out what type of crops are most in demand.
- Talk to your competitors and see whether they could be potential customers.
- Try test-trading if possible.

CHAPTER 4

Essential equipment

So now you have somewhere to grow your produce; you've also done some market research, and you have a good idea of where your customers are going to come from and what they are looking for. The next stage is to work out what equipment you will need in order to start growing veg and really get the business going. In contrast to some businesses, you'll most likely have a large outlay while starting up (capital costs for equipment and so on), which will drop after the first year or so, depending on your plans for business growth. But your running costs compared with those of many other businesses will be relatively low (seed or young plants, compost, packaging and sundries), although of course this will depend on what you grow and also on any rent agreements. Bear in mind that the bulk of your yearly expenses may come in just a month or two in spring, when your cash flow may be slow owing to your having little available produce to sell.

While all of the equipment described in this chapter will of course be cheaper if bought second-hand, some things really do have to be bought new – such as polytunnel plastic, which cannot be reused if an old tunnel is taken down and moved elsewhere. Car boot sales are great places for finding second-hand garden equipment such as forks and spades, as are house clearances and auction houses. Websites such as eBay and Freecycle can also be good sources, and check specialist growers' and gardeners' web forums.

Equipment for growing

Many gardeners and growers will be familiar with most of this equipment, and it's easy to overlook the cost of everyday items such as spades, forks and seed trays in favour of larger purchases such as polytunnels and tractors. However, it's worth making an equipment checklist, otherwise you could find that you'll be missing some obvious tools, and have to go on a shopping splurge which could blow your monthly budget in one go.

Crop protection

Polytunnels and greenhouses are not essential to a market garden business, but they are definitely desirable. Although they can be expensive to buy and set up, you can grow a whole range of more valuable and marketable crops in them. And, because crops are protected, they are generally more productive than exposed plants (especially in winter). Putting up a polytunnel or greenhouse can be a headache, but if new it should come with instructions, and there are also several good guides online, and advice on forums. It's useful to have someone who has some experience in putting up polytunnels on hand during the frame construction and 'skinning' stages; try contacting your local growers' group or your tunnel supplier for advice. You need a still, warm day to put the plastic skin on the tunnel, and as many volunteers as possible.

If you want to raise your own plant seedlings, you'll definitely need a warm sheltered construction that allows the light in, such as a module tunnel or greenhouse, or at the very least (for smaller market gardens) some heated propagation boxes and sunny windowsills at home. These can be home-made: various methods use a range of components, such as heated mats or fluorescent tubes (the light and heat from the latter is just enough to get things started); plans and guides for these are available online for free. As long as you have a heat source – even if just the sun and a way of keeping to the minimum required temperature for 24 hours a day – germination should be simple.

You might also want to consider pest-proof fencing, such as rabbit fencing for any unprotected beds, or deer fencing for fields if you have a severe cervine problem (these will need to be 1.8m high to keep acrobatic fallow deer out; roe and muntjac deer should at least think twice at 1.5m fences). If you're near woodland and have badgers in the area, you'll also probably need electric fencing when growing tempting crops such as sweetcorn – badgers often plough through standard fencing to get at these favourites.

Don't forget that rabbit fencing will also need a trench on the outside of the fence, with a foot or so of the wire fencing laid out horizontally in it, to prevent rabbits from digging underneath the fence. If you have a serious rabbit problem, it might be worth tracking down a local ferret or terrier owner; ferret scent will also keep rabbits away for a couple of weeks once ferrets have been in their burrows, even if no rabbits are caught.

Wood recycling yards are a good source of cheaper (and greener) fence posts, baton and other bits and pieces you might need for making propagating tables or benches, doors and so on. If there are any woodland management or forestry businesses nearby, they might be willing to swap poles and planks for a helping hand (they could also be a supplier of soil-improving charcoal finings and other handy by-products such as woodchip for paths or composting).

Pigeons are the scourge of organic growers: they can decimate brassicas and other crops in a day. Physical barriers such as nets do a good job (Enviromesh is probably the best at protecting against a range of pests), but can be a pain to take off and put back on again when harvesting or weeding; as an alternative, bird-scaring gas guns and other mechanisms that make noises are pretty effective. A cheaper (although perhaps less efficacious) option is a home-made scarecrow, or a selection of shiny objects such as CDs arranged to wave in the wind on strings. You could also try an air rifle for some free pigeon meat or just to scare them away; remember to observe the law, though (take 'reasonable precautions' to prevent anyone under the age of 18 from gaining unauthorised access to your gun; ensure you have permission from the landowner or person with the sporting rights and that you know precisely where the boundaries are; don't fire within 15m of the centre of a highway), and ensure you're well away from livestock and footpaths.

Fleece is lighter than netting and used mostly for protecting crops from late or early frosts, although it can also be useful as a barrier to pests. Unlike nets, fleece tends to last for only a season or two, especially if used outdoors in all weathers rather than in polytunnels, because it rips easily. Mice also helpfully like to chew it up to make nests. You'll need some heavy items to keep fleece and nets in place: you can buy specially made pegs for nets, or make your own with wire. For fleece, weighted sand or stone bags are a better option, because it will tear with pegs. You could make your own bags using compost sacks and stones, tied round the neck to keep closed, but these last only a year or two as the plastic perishes when exposed to the elements. UV-stabilised materials, such as spare polytunnel plastic, last longer.

Propagating

Unless you are sowing all your crops directly in the ground, you will need some sowing and potting-on compost (or a multipurpose mix). Until you get up and running, it's likely that you'll need to buy some compost in for the first year at least. There are various peat-free organically approved composts on the market now (or ones made from sustainably collected peat, washed up downriver of peat bogs), and your choice may depend on the crop planned. Coir-based composts will need careful watering, since the long fibres tend to send most of the water away, plus the top can look dry when underneath the compost is already damp, and vice versa. You may find that some composts have weed seeds in them, although sterilised options are available. Green-waste composts, made from garden waste, are pretty sustainable, but also tend to be quite woody and can suffer from sciarid fly problems.

You could mix up your own blend of sowing compost using various combinations of inert leafmould or woodchip compost; something like sand, vermiculite or perlite for good drainage; plus some nutrient content such as an organic feed, composted green waste or manure, or compost 'teas' such as comfrey, nettle or seaweed.

Green-waste composts can also be a good source of fertility for the soil and help put loads of organic matter in the ground quickly: ideal for light, sandy soils or those that aren't currently best for horticulture – especially if you're not using manures. If you don't have enough in your own compost heap, contact your local council to find out how much they charge for delivering a lorry-load – many will sell by the bag too.

If you are propagating your own plants, you will also want seed trays or modules and pots, plant labels and a waterproof pen or pencil. These last items are more important than they might seem: it's sometimes difficult to keep track of varieties and sowing dates to see how well they are performing.

Indoor propagation will also require benches or tables for module and seed trays: these can be found cheaply or for free from recycling sites, or easily made at home using old pallets on top of shortened fence posts or other sturdy legs, with some wooden baton triangles between the legs to add stability.

You will probably already have an idea of the kinds of crops you want to grow, and hopefully a rough plan of quantities: whether little-and-often sowings, such as salads, or bulk maincrops, sown all in one go, such as squashes and carrots. It's worth calculating approximately how much each crop will cost in terms of seed (or plants if buying in), by working out how much of each crop seed you will need: in general, allow for less than 100-per-cent germination rates (parsnips, in particular, have at best a 72-per-cent germination rate), pest problems and other mishaps. The spacing you choose and therefore the total amount of seed you need for each crop may depend on the variety you want and will also depend on the size of crop you are aiming for – you can fit twice as much in if you plan to sell small 'baby' leeks or salad, for example, than if the same plants are harvested as a maincrop, which will need wider spacings.

It's sometimes worth shopping around for seeds and plants, since several companies may offer different

Seed used on my own 2-acre garden in 2013

Crop	Variety	Supplier (or own saved seed)
Aubergines	Falcon F1	Tamar
Beans, broad	Hangdown Green	Tamar
	Super Aquadulce	Tamar
	Supersimonia	Tamar
Beans, French climbing	Blauhilde	Tamar
	Cobra	Tamar
	Neckargold	Tamar
Beans, French dwarf	Faraday	Tamar
	Helios	Tamar
	Purple Teepee	Tuckers
Beetroot	Alvro Mono	Tamar
	Bolivar Detroit	Tamar
	Chioggia	Tamar
	Golden Detroit	Tamar

prices on the same product. Organic seed is usually more expensive, owing to the higher production costs. A simple spreadsheet listing crops, quantities needed, supplier and price will help ensure you haven't missed anything, and you can also then remind yourself of the varieties that did well for you, for reference when ordering seed the following year. The table on the following pages gives an example of some popular crops – those I used in my 2-acre garden in 2013. Seed is usually quite cheap (apart from F1 hybrid seeds), so it's worth getting too much rather than too little, in case you suddenly have room for more, or the first crop fails.

Quantity (seeds/pills, grams or packet)	Cost	Organic seed (O) or conventional (C)
25(s)	£6.00	O
500g	£8.10	O
1kg	£8.00	O
500g	£5.00	O
pkt	£1.60	O
pkt	£1.60	O
pkt	£1.60	O
250g	£7.60	O
250g	£8.75	O
1kg	£9.00	C
5,000(s)	£18.15	O
100g	£13.00	O
50g	£7.40	O
30g	£10.80	O

Broccoli	Early White Sprouting	Tuckers
	PSB Early	Tamar
	Santee	Tamar
	Summer Purple	Tuckers
Cabbage	January King: Deadon F1	Tamar
	Savoy: Marner Grufewi	Tamar
	Savoy: Vorbote 3 / Hilmar	Tamar
	Spring cabbage: Pixie	Tamar
Calabrese	Belstar F1	Tamar
	Green Sprouting	Tamar
Carrots	Amsterdam Forcing	Tamar
	Napoli	Tuckers
	Purple Haze	Tuckers
	Rainbow	Tuckers
	White Satin	Tamar
Celeriac	Prinz	Tamar
Celery	Tall Utah	Tamar
Chard / leaf beet	Rainbow Chard	Tamar
	Ruby chard: Vulkan	Tamar
Chicory	Pan de Sucre	Tamar
	Rossa Treviso	Tamar
Coriander	Filtro	Tamar
Courgettes	Cocozelle (stripey)	Tamar
	Nero di Milano	Tamar
	Partenon F1	Tamar
Cress	Bubbles	CN Seeds
Cucumbers	Marketmore	Tamar
	Melen F1	Tamar
	Styx F1 (long)	Tamar
Endive	Markant	Tamar
	Pancalieri	Tamar
Fennel	Fino	Tamar

10g	£6.00	C
pkt	£1.10	O
250(s)	£12.00	C
2,000(s)	£6.00	O
2g [250(s)]	£8.15	O
2g	£3.15	O
pkt [100(s)]	£1.60	O
pkt	£1.10	O
500(s)	£8.50	O
pkt	£1.10	O
25g	£7.25	O
5,000(s)	£8.50	O
5,000(s)	£8.50	C
5,000(s)	£8.50	C
5,000(s)	£5.95	O
1g [500(s)]	£4.95	O
1g	£3.00	O
600(s)	£4.05	O
25g	£4.95	O
25g	£3.00	O
25g	£3.00	O
100g	£6.00	O
pkt [10(s)]	£1.10	O
25g	£3.60	O
25(s)	£5.95	O
50g	£3.80	C
pkt	£1.10	O
pkt [5(s)]	£3.05	O
pkt	£3.60	O
2g	£3.50	O
10g	£2.40	O
10g	£4.50	O

Fenugreek	Fenugreek	CN Seeds
Garlic	Thermidrome	Saved
Good King Henry	Good King Henry	Tuckers
Kale	Halbhoher Grun Krauser	Tamar
	Nero di Toscana	Tamar
	Westland Winter	Tamar
Leeks	Autumn Mammoth 2 Hannibal	Tamar
	Axima	Tamar
	Bandit	Tamar
	Zermatt	Tamar
Lettuce	Baby lollo rossa: Redlo	Tamar
	Baby oak green: Oaking	Tamar
	Baby oak red: Sadawi	Tamar
	Batavia: Leny	Tuckers
	Batavia: Mohican RZ	Tuckers
	Red cos: Cegolaine RZ	Tuckers
Parsley	French Giant	Tamar
	Japanese parsley: Mitsuba	CN Seeds
Parsley root	Hamburg	CN Seeds
Parsnips	Halblange White	Tuckers
	Pixie	Tuckers
Peas	Progress No. 9	Tuckers
Peppers, chilli	Cayenne / Ring of Fire	Saved
Peppers, sweet	Long Red Marconi	Tamar
	Yolo Wonder	Tamar
Salad bags (winter)	Beetroot: Bulls Blood	Tamar
	Claytonia / winter purslane	Tamar
	Corn salad: D'Orlanda	Tamar
	Mibuna	Tamar
	Mizuna	Tamar
	Mustard: Giant Red	Tamar
	Mustard: Golden Frills	Tamar
	Mustard: Green in Snow	Tamar

250g	£3.60	C
1kg		
pkt	£1.70	C
pkt	£1.10	O
pkt	£1.10	O
250(s)	£3.25	O
10g	£5.50	O
1,000(s)	£3.50	O
2,000(s)	£9.00	O
1,000(s)	£4.60	O
5,000(s)	£4.50	O
5,000(s)	£4.50	O
5,000(s)	£4.50	O
1g	£7.00	O
100(p)	£6.00	O
100(p)	£6.00	O
50g	£5.75	O
10g	£2.45	C
50g	£4.05	C
50g	£8.50	O
2,000(s)	£10.00	O
1kg	£7.25	O
20(s)		
pkt [30(s)]	£1.35	O
pkt [30(s)]	£1.35	O
25g	£3.50	O
900(s)	£1.35	O
500(s)	£1.10	O
500(s)	£1.10	O
400(s)	£1.10	O
500(s)	£1.10	O
400(s)	£1.35	O
400(s)	£1.10	O

	Pak choi: Tai Sai	Tamar
Spinach	Renegade F1	Tamar
Squashes/pumpkins	Baby Bear	Tuckers
	Buttercup	Tamar
	Crown Prince F1	Tuckers
	Fictor F1	Tamar
Sweetcorn	Earligold	Tuckers
Tomatoes, beefsteak	Berner Rose	Tamar
	Brandy Wine	Tuckers
Tomatoes, cherry	Black Cherry	CN Seeds
	Gardener's Delight	Tamar
Tomatoes, vine	Cindel F1	Tamar
	Golden Queen	Tamar
	Green Zebra	Tuckers
	Tigerella	Tuckers
Herbs	Basil: Nufar	Tamar
	Chives: Staro	Tamar
	Dill	Tamar
	French sorrel	Tamar
	Green mint	CN Seeds
	Mexican tarragon	CN Seeds
	Summer savory	Tamar
	Thyme	Tamar
	Winter savory	Tamar
Flowers	Delphiniums: Magic Fountain Mix	CN Seeds
	Eryngium Bourgatii	CN Seeds
	Nasturtiums	Tamar + saved
	Scabious	CN Seeds
	Sweet peas: Old Spice	Tamar
	Marigolds (calendula)	Saved
	Marigolds (tagetes): Orange	Tamar
Total		

250(s)	£1.10	O
10,000(s)	£5.75	O
100(s)	£5.00	C
50(s)	£3.00	O
50(s)	£5.50	O
50(s)	£3.30	O
1,000(s)	£6.00	C
pkt	£1.10	O
pkt	£1.50	C
100(s)	£5.65	C
1g	£4.00	O
25(s)	£3.40	O
pkt	£1.10	O
pkt [25(s)]	£2.00	C
2g	£5.00	C
10g	£3.50	O
pkt	£1.10	O
pkt	£1.10	O
pkt	£1.10	O
1g	£2.00	C
1g	£2.25	C
pkt	£1.10	O
pkt	£1.10	O
pkt	£1.10	O
250(s)	£2.50	C
100(s)	£1.90	C
25g	£4.00	O
25(s)	£3.45	C
10g	£3.25	O
10g		
pkt	£1.35	O
	£458.00	

Irrigation

Given the number of terribly wet summers over recent years in the UK, it's easy to forget that crops will need watering in dry periods – even in winter for protected crops. While this might be less important for outdoor crops unless a really dry spell occurs, irrigation is paramount for indoor crops. Leafy produce in particular will not tolerate dry conditions, and will quickly run to seed. Watering by hand with a can or hose, from either a tap or water butts, is probably the cheapest option if you have the time, but for larger polytunnels or protected areas it's a good idea to install some piped irrigation, which not only saves time but also prevents soil compaction from walking around.

A simple overhead sprinkler system is not difficult to set up for leafy produce, but will require a consistent level of water pressure, while drip hoses running along the ground are good for crops that prefer not to get wet leaves (such as tomatoes, which are susceptible to blight in damp conditions), and usually require less water pressure. A basic overhead system will consist of simply a length of pipe, attached securely to crop bars or supported wires, running from a tap, with a stopper on the end. Sprinkler heads can be inserted at intervals along the pipe. You can also install a cheap timer at the water source to ensure crops get irrigated when you're not there.

Outside systems are based on the same principle: either drip, trickle-tape or porous hose lengths with a stopper at one end, or stands with sprinkler heads attached to them, placed at intervals along a length of piping.

Tools and sundries

It's easy to get carried away when buying tools: any new gadget always seems like that ideal labour-saving device you've been looking for! However, as one grower told me, the best tools you can ever own are your hands. Anything else is therefore a bonus! You will need the familiar gardening basics at least: a wheelbarrow, hoe(s), watering can, spade, fork, rake, trowel and dibber; plus various hardware for any DIY, such as a hammer, saw, drill, wire cutters, pliers and so on. You'll want lots of gloves too, of course, to look after those most precious tools in winter or for weeding aggressive weeds. If you have a couple of acres or more, it's also worth investing in a wheelhoe: a well-designed hand tool with a metal blade attached to a wheel and two handles, to make weeding much easier. It would probably also help to have some kind of seeder mechanism, so you can sow large numbers of seeds in the ground in straight lines. The cheapest and easiest for small-scale growers is probably the EarthWay seeder, which comes with a range of plates for differently sized seeds. However, the range of market garden tools is growing all the time, especially from the US and mainland Europe, so shop around.

Depending on the crops you are growing, you might also need stakes, canes or netting for climbing plants to grow up; a lawnmower and/or strimmer or scythe for keeping paths, edges and green manures under control; and baskets and knives, shears or scissors for harvesting. You may want to grow crops through ground-cover fabric such as Mypex, to keep weeds down in some areas; note that the best way to make holes for planting through this thin plastic woven membrane is with a heated poker or gas torch, to melt the plastic edges and prevent the fabric fraying over time. Mypex can be pinned down with special barbed pegs, or – a cheaper option – small wire hoops or sandbags.

If you're not using the no-dig method of adding plenty of compost and allowing worms to incorporate it rather than physically turning over the soil yourself, you may want to invest in a plough and/or rotovator. A two-wheeled pedestrian rotovator will do a lot of work and a good job, but if you have an acre or so to culti-vate at a time, a tractor-mounted machine does a better job in a much shorter time and with less effort. Use of a tractor is a great advantage, and other attach-ments such as tines for weeding, a root-crop harvester, a ridger and a trailer are also labour-savers. However, if you only have an acre or so, it's hard to justify the expense of buying or renting a tractor. It's possible to buy larger and more expensive equipment between a group of local growers or gardeners, of course, but bear in mind that you will probably all want to use it at the same time! Some market gardeners use horse- or donkey-power for cultivating, weeding and moving produce around, which also saves on fuel, but you'll need some training and specialist equipment in order to use them effectively.

Other business essentials

The equipment you need for a market garden doesn't stop at the tools and structures for growing the produce. What about packaging the crops, moving them around, and communicating to your customers when the produce is ready?

Packaging

Many crops, especially cut leaves such as salads, or delicate produce such as tomatoes and strawberries, will need some kind of packaging, no matter who your customers are. There is a wide range on offer: from paper and plastic bags to punnets and wooden, cardboard or plastic boxes. Some packaging options are more eco-friendly than others: corn-starch bags, for example (however, although undoubtedly more environmentally responsible than normal clear plastic bags, they do tend to suck all the moisture out of the crops inside – plus, customers can't see inside the bags, so they're not great for shop sales). Recycled, reusable and recyclable packaging is available, but takes a little more hunting down and costs more money than the mainstream options. For direct or shop sales, it's also worth making sure that bags of leaves or unfamiliar and unusual crops are labelled somehow, either directly on a bag or box or tagged. You could also include your logo and contact details on packaging such as cardboard veg boxes or reusable bags, making it into an extra marketing tool.

You may also need some larger bags or boxes for packing orders into. For local and small-scale deliveries, it's simple to obtain cardboard and wooden crates from shops and supermarkets. If you'll be selling a large amount of produce, however, you may want your own uniform boxes for delivery.

For selling crops by weight, rather than by number of items, you'll need some accurate scales. Electronic scales are more precise for smaller weights, and can be found from a range of sources, including specialist shops and dealers.

Transport

Selling your produce on-site from the garden gate cuts down the expense of transport, and can also reduce packaging, but this is not always possible – or at least not for all your produce. There are also other benefits from keeping deliveries local: delivering on foot with a hand-cart will get you noticed (and very fit!), as will delivering by bike or horse with a pull-along cart. Some enterprising entrepreneurs in Mumbai deliver lunches to office workers via train using special set tins and backpacks, which is an interesting idea if your local rail network is near your customers, reliable and reasonably priced.

If these ideas are impractical for your location and set-up, a suitable car or van may be necessary – and you might want to think about whether you need a chiller compartment for longer journeys in the summer. If you're not in a position to buy a van at this stage, you could consider the option of leasing one, which might be a good way of trying out deliveries before committing to a large outlay. However, leasing will mean that you won't be able to take advantage of the van's exterior to advertise your business (unless you use removable magnetic logos).

Communication

You will, of course, need some way for your customers and suppliers to get in touch with you. The most obvious requirement is a telephone: a mobile is preferable, whether in addition to a landline or not, so you can be contacted when out and about. A postal address is also essential, for invoices to be sent to, and to register your bank and tax information. You'll need a computer: to keep basic accounts, to communicate by email (whether or not you intend to take orders that way), and perhaps to produce some marketing information. You'll also need to upload updates if you have a website, blog or social media business account (see Chapter 9 for more about marketing). A Smartphone is especially useful, since it will allow you to check any emails on the go too. All of these methods of communication can be based at your home, with your personal computer and existing telephone; just keep records of the proportion of time you spend using them for business matters, so you can claim back these costs against taxable income (see Chapter 6).

Equipment checklist

The checklist in the table below and overleaf is based on the essentials I needed when starting up my 2-acre market garden; this should give a rough idea of costs when budgeting for your project. Most of the equip-

Start-up equipment for a 2-acre market garden

Equipment
Polytunnel, 5.5x16m: steel frame, fittings & wooden door frames
Polytunnel skin / cladding plastic & anti-hotspot tape
Polytunnel doors per tunnel: wooden batten, leftover polytunnel plastic & fixings
Enviromesh: 1.35mm mesh, 13x50m roll
Fleece roll: 18gm, 2x100m
Net/fleece weights (stones/bricks in leftover polytunnel plastic)
Black woven ground-cover fabric (Mypex/Phormisol): 105gm roll, 3.3x100m
Irrigation for one polytunnel (both sprinkler system & drip-hose system)
Irrigation for field: field stands, sprinkler heads, pipe & tap for moveable 50m sprinkler strip

ment in this list was bought from new, but some items, such as garden tools, were bought second-hand, and others, such as the polytunnel doors, were home-made. The prices in the table don't include delivery charges from suppliers: some don't charge for delivery if the total order is over a minimum price; on the other hand, delivery charges may be substantial if you're not buying from a local source (for example, £100 when buying heavy or large items such as Enviromesh netting from the other end of the country). It makes sense to split orders with other local growers whenever possible and practical.

New, second-hand or home-made	Approximate cost (inc. VAT)
New	£900
New	£275
Home-made	£40
Second-hand	£135
New	£32
Home-made	£0
New	£145
New	£200
New	£190

Timer for tunnel irrigation

Fencing: wire fencing (25mm mesh, 0.9x25m rolls), stakes, wire & hog rings for 215m rabbit-proof fence

Rotovator (1960s Howard 350)

EarthWay seeder & extra plates

Lawnmower (Honda Izy)

Strimmer and brushcutter

Garden tools: spade, rake, fork, hoe, watering can, wheelbarrow, stakes, trowels, stepladder, shears

Propagation tables: $1m^2$, 0.8m high x 6

Electric propagating unit

Sowing compost: 70-litre bags x 10

Green-waste compost: approx. 6 tonnes

Rigid plastic module trays (150 cells per tray) x 50

Sundries: plant labels, string, polytunnel repair tape, nails & screws, etc.

Small gas torch

Digital retail scales (30kg limit)

Plastic punnets & lids: 1kg capacity, case of 1,000

Plastic degradable bags: 150 gauge, 23x30cm, box of 5,000

Cardboard/wooden delivery boxes

Budgeting

As can be seen from my set-up costs, for a basic market garden on a couple of acres it's advisable to budget for at least £4,000 for equipment. Plus, as we saw from the table on pages 52-59, you would need to set aside around £400+ for seed or plant costs for an acre or two

New	£50
New	£420
Second-hand	£280
New	£180
Second-hand	£60
New	£145
Second-hand	£300
Home-made	£36
New	£30
New	£62
New	£260
New	£125
New	£200
New	£25
New	£80
New	£135
New	£130
Second-hand	£0

Total: £4,435

of land too, although of course this will depend on what you want to grow and how much of each crop. (For future years, saving seed can help cut down costs, as well as producing robust varieties well suited to your conditions.) Other running costs to bear in mind are any land rents or charges (including bank charges and any interest on loans), water, electricity, council rates (if not included in any rent), insurance and any labour.

If you are working alone and can afford it, you may be able to work for yourself for free for the first year, ploughing any money from sales back into the business. If you need to employ someone, however, you will also need to budget for this. Volunteers can be invaluable when setting up a business – and are also a great way of including the local community in your project. You might be surprised at how enthusiastic and knowledgeable your community is, and how willing some people are to work for a project they really believe in, where they can meet like-minded people, learn some useful skills and be part of something – all for the price of lunch and perhaps a pint later.

In total it would be sensible to budget for at least £5,000 initially to get a business on 2 acres up and running in the first year. The more land you have, the less per acre your costs will be as capital expenses such as equipment will be spread over a larger area, so for a higher acreage you'd expect to spend below £2,500 per acre, depending of course on the costs of any large investments such as tractors and barns. Similarly, a smaller scale than 2 acres may incur more than £2,500/acre in capital costs. Depending on your set-up and how successful your first season is, that may well be all you need before you start covering future costs, and even start paying yourself.

Equipment checklist

- Draw up your desired equipment list.
- Try to keep costs down by finding second-hand equipment, sharing resources with other growers, and making your own where appropriate and possible.
- If putting up a polytunnel, plan the construction for a time when you're not so busy, perhaps in winter or early spring, and round up some volunteers on a sunny still day to skin it with the plastic.
- Decide whether you'd like to make your own compost, or buy it in; or concentrate more on directly sown crops and buy in ready-grown plants when needed.
- Think about whether you'd rather spend more on eco-friendly packaging.
- Consider whether some innovative delivery options would be feasible.
- Try saving seed to keep costs down, and breed your own robust varieties.
- Keep a close eye on your budget throughout.

CHAPTER 5

Raising the money

The financing required will of course depend on the size of business planned, but for anything more than the smallest of enterprises, and unless you're lucky enough to have savings or another good income that enables you to pay for all your expenses, you'll need to find extra funding from somewhere. As we saw in the previous chapter, for a couple of acres the start-up costs for your first year might be in the region of £5,000 – though this is really a shoestring budget and assumes that you're able to get a number of tools second-hand, and also to make some things yourself. A budget of £10,000 over two years is more realistic for your expenses (although you will have made sales by then, which could cover some of these costs) – and don't forget that this doesn't include paying for your time, or that of anyone else you employ.

Sources of funding

Don't be put off by the idea of having to raise funds for your project. Financial matters can seem daunting, but in fact you will find that there are many sources of financing available – from private funding or loans from patrons, investors or banks to community initiatives, government schemes and charity grants.

Private funding

It is possible to find benefactors, entrepreneurs or patrons who believe in local and sustainable food projects, and who might be willing to sponsor your idea and foot the bill for your start-up costs and perhaps even for your time for the first year or so. This might be in the form of a one-off payment or grant, if they're really keen and affluent; or a loan, which you'll have to pay back once the business starts making money. If you do go down the private funding route, ensure that there are clear understandings and contracts in place: in particular, regarding who owns what, the interest rates on any loans, and what the patron's motivations and expectations are compared with your own.

Private or corporate funders can be excellent partners in business, but if either party involved isn't used to business arrangements it can be difficult to delineate what the deal really is, and what would happen in the event of a disagreement or problem with the business. If they demanded their money back within the month,

for example, could you cope? If not, make sure the contract includes a realistic notice period on either side, such as a minimum of three or six months. Don't feel embarrassed about asking for a formal contract or agreement: it will mean that both sides know exactly where they stand, and will prevent misunderstandings or worse down the line.

Banks

If taking on an agreement with unknown private investors seems a bit daunting, you could turn to an ethical bank for a loan – the bank thereby acting as the organiser and intermediary between you, the business, and them, the investors. Banks such as Triodos and the Co-operative specialise in offering savings and investment accounts to ethically minded customers, who like to see their money put to good use in the form of bank loans to sustainable and ethical businesses. Some accounts might have conditions: they might want to see that you are certified organic, for example, or growing on a minimum amount of land. Any investor or bank will want to see a watertight business plan (see page 80), but they will help and give you guidance to achieve this, so it's definitely worth looking into. Just keep any interest rates and other conditions in mind when budgeting.

Most other major banks also have loans available for small start-ups too, of course: shop around and compare interest rates and other conditions or penalties. You may prefer not to be associated with a bank that has dubious ethical credentials – paying them interest on your loan for them to invest elsewhere, perhaps in something you don't approve of. However, if the interest rates are very competitive, you may feel you have little choice. Take the time to research your options in order to make the best choice for your business.

Community support

If you want to go down the Community Supported Agriculture (CSA) route, how you find funding will be part of how that model works. Some schemes will have customers paying up-front to join the scheme, before any produce has even been sown, which will provide a fund to draw on for equipment expenses and so on. There are many different CSA models, and you could also construct your own – the basic idea simply being that of a community coming together to produce food for itself. Draw up a budget and a business plan, to help you work out how much money you'll need to start with (and also how the project will eventually fund itself), then get your partners on the committee to help you start fundraising.

If the various models and benefits of CSAs don't appeal to you, you can still try fundraising in your local community to get you started. The idea of having a good, sustainable local food producer could be so appealing that many people may want to donate or fund the start-up anyway, without expecting a share, a stake in or a commitment to the business longer term. Or you could offer some 'rewards' to those who pledge money to help you get started: such as their first month's boxes of veg free, a roll of honour included on your website or blog, or even a plaque on your polytunnel if they donate a large amount!

The CSA Network offers training days or courses and other community support. Even if you're not part of a CSA scheme, as long as your business has a community angle you could approach the CSA Network, the Soil Association, or Making Local Food Work directly for guidance and support.

Crowdfunding

The internet has provided a revolution in crowdfunding and peer-to-peer lending: along similar lines to the local-community-fundraising ideas above, websites such as Kickstarter and Buzzbnk allow potential businesses and projects to pitch to a worldwide audience. These sites work as follows: you put together your proposal for a project or business, with a goal of however much you think you need to get going (for example £10,000). You then offer tiers of rewards to anyone who pledges: for instance, a donor pledges £10 online and gets a box of vegetables in your first season (you can stipulate that rewards such as these are available only to people in a certain delivery area); £50 and they get the free veg box plus an email newsletter every month; £100 and they get these rewards plus a special invite to your launch party and so on. Anyone at all can pledge online through the website; if you fail to hit your target by your deadline, any money pledged is returned to the donors, so you won't get any money at all if you miss your target – but you won't have to fulfil any of the rewards either.

Crowdfunding is an excellent way to raise money and awareness, while not being dependent on one or two major funders, and retain ownership of your project. This style of funding can raise huge sums too: some of Barack Obama's original election success was down to a vast amount of small donations rather than several enormous ones. However, you must be sure that you can meet the rewards. It's possible to limit the number of rewards in a given tier, which also provides an incentive to interested people to pledge sooner rather than later. If a certain reward tier does sell out, people can carry on donating anyway, just without the rewards, and if you hit your target early, pledges will still be accepted until the deadline day, so you may raise more money than you'd expected. You might also find that you get pledges from far afield from people who don't expect a reward even if they are in time for one, but just like your idea.

Trusts and charities

There is a surprising number of trusts and charities around the UK (and within the EU) that have been set up to help sustainable and food-related businesses get started. This perhaps shows both the desire and the demand among the public for good local food, which is not supported by current economic and environmental policies. These charities are usually very keen to support local and sustainable projects such as community market gardens, but it can be difficult to find out about what funding may available.

Some trusts will fund only registered charities, and finding funding from trusts and charities is almost a job in itself. However, it is worth having at least a look to see if you'd be eligible for some finance to help with your start-up costs. A charity or project that offers other benefits alongside food production, such as education or farming for disabled groups, can attract several potential funding sources. Do remember, though, that you will probably be looking to make the food-production business the main source of your income, rather than relying on grants or charity funding, so you'll need to charge a sustainable amount for your produce. You never know when charity funding might run out.

If you are a charity, you can also apply for local or national government grants for various aspects of your business: for example, offering training or work for the unemployed, or conservation work. Contact your local council to find out more about local projects and schemes, and whether there is any financial support available.

One fund of particular use for potential growers under the age of 31 is the Prince's Trust Kanabus Fund: this has grants and low-interest loans available for any start-up business involved in farming or horticulture. Grants of up to £2,250 are available, along with low-interest loans of up to £10,000, following completion of the free four-day business course and presentation of a detailed business plan to a panel of trustees. You'll also be provided with a business mentor for two years. To find out more about the fund, contact your regional Prince's Trust office directly.

Other funding

While it may not always be possible to find direct funding when setting up your business (and the golden days of government funding for worthy projects may well be over, for now at least), there are various schemes that could help in other ways. Lantra is the UK's Sector Skills Council for land-based and environmental industries, and offers guidance and links to funded training and learning. The Skills Funding Agency can also help point you in the direction of training programmes and bursaries. If you decide to take part in more training or higher education before starting your business, there are also special bursaries and trusts available for courses relating to horticulture or food production, but they can be difficult to track down until you know where you'd like to study. Some agricultural colleges are able to run subsidised short courses, so contact any colleges local to you and subscribe to their mailing lists to find out more.

DEFRA (the Department for Environment, Food & Rural Affairs) also administers the Entry Level and Organic Entry Level Stewardship schemes: if you own or manage land, you can claim £30/ha/year, or £60/ha/year for organic land, if you meet the criteria. The aim is to support the farming and managing of land in an environmentally friendly and responsible way: if you're planning to be organic, or to grow food in an uncertified but still generally sustainable way, you will probably find it very easy to follow the scheme's demands.

The Welsh Assembly Government has historically been very supportive of organic and sustainable farms, and has offered financial support and incentives as well as ongoing guidance and training. The Scottish Government has money set aside too for its Rural Development Plan, so it's worth finding out if your business might be eligible for help. Northern Ireland's Department of Agriculture and Rural Development (DARD) organic farming scheme offers financial aid to farmers and growers in converting to organic farming.

Making a business plan

No matter where your funding is coming from, you'll need a business plan. Even if you're able to fund the business yourself or with other private finance, a business plan is a great way to lay out exactly what it is that you plan to do, grow and sell, and to make sure you've taken all the business aspects such as finance, competition and marketing into consideration. It's also a very good idea to run through how the business will work on a practical level: considering possible pitfalls and how you will deal with them will give you confidence to go ahead. It will also help you decide whether you want to take on help, or start on your own for now.

Business plans vary enormously, and there are a large number of different templates to help you besides the example given overleaf – have a look online for some examples of different formats. Just like CVs, business plans come in all shapes and sizes: particular banks or charities who require a plan may have specific sections they want you to cover, but in general plans should include what the business actually is (for instance, a market garden), your goals and how you will achieve them, and an executive summary. Not only is a business plan not just for the bank or funding source (you will find it useful yourself to write down your plans), but it's not set in stone either. Obstacles are bound to occur of course, and will mean that you deviate from your plan to a greater or lesser extent, but if you keep updating your plan as life (and the weather) throws up unexpected challenges, you'll be able to cope and adapt much more easily.

Basic business plan

1. **Business details**
   Your business name, address and contact details;
   your name and home address.

2. **Executive summary**
   2a) Business summary
   A brief overview of what your business will do;
   who you will sell to; the business status (sole
   trader, partnership, limited company or charity /
   not-for-profit group – *see Chapter 6*); where your
   funding will come from.

   2b) Business aims
   What you want to achieve in the short, medium
   and long term.

   2c) Financial summary
   Your projected costing for starting up and running
   costs, and any more details on how you plan to
   fund the business.

3. **Business owner's background**
   Why you want to run your own business; previous
   work experience; qualifications, education and
   training; relevant hobbies and interests.

4. **The product**
   Why your product is important; any other products (e.g. herbs, flowers, plants, training, courses)
   you will offer; when and where the produce will be

sold (you could include a rough table of seasons, with what you'll be selling in spring, summer, autumn and winter); whether you'll be picking and selling from fresh or storing produce.

5. **The market**
Whether you'll be selling to businesses or individuals; wholesale or retail, or a mixture; examples of planned sales outlets; examples of customer demand / expressions of interest; where your customers are, what they are looking for, and why they will buy your produce.

6. **Market research**
Desk and field research; results of any test-trading; who and where your competition is, including strengths and weaknesses of each competitor; SWOT analysis (strengths and weaknesses of, opportunities for and threats to) the proposed business; the business's USP (unique selling point) (*see Chapter 3*).

7. **Marketing strategy**
Plans for marketing, such as word of mouth, leaflets, business cards, advertising, website, social networking, promotional campaigns, open days, samples; costs of marketing and advertising (*see Chapter 9*).

8. **Logistics**
How the business will run; how crops will be produced and delivered (where the premises are, tools needed, any packaging or storage); how customers

will pay you (for instance, will you need a card machine, or will you stick to cash, cheques and online payments?); example suppliers and equipment needed; transport; any legal and insurance requirements; any plans for extra staff.

9. **Pricing and forecasts**

Examples of produce pricing (retail and wholesale if different) and how prices are calculated (market comparison, cost of production, profit margin and mark-ups – although this is very tricky and, for vegetables, tends in practice to be ad hoc; it might help to have a rough idea of what you need/want to add on top of crop production costs – *see Chapter 8*); forecast yield for the following year; forecast cash flow for the following year; sales and expenses forecast for the next year; estimated turnover.

10. **Joy**

Business plans can be a pretty dry affair, but there's nothing to stop you including some photos or drawings to help illustrate what you're trying to say – at the very least it will probably cheer you up a bit while you're writing the plan!

Raising the money checklist

- Work out where your start-up money is coming from. Have you got enough of your own savings to get going? Do you know any private investors who may be interested? Will you need a bank loan? Would community funding suit you? Are there any relevant grants available for your particular business model and location?

- Think too about how you will pay back any loans. What are your commitments, both financial (interest repayments and so on) and produce based (for instance, rewards on a crowdfunding website such as Kickstarter, or veg boxes for a CSA)? Are both realistic?

- Make a business plan. Include as much detail as possible about the local and national market, your plans for the business, and how you will make the business financially sustainable once your start-up money runs out.

- Work out the practicalities and logistics of how the business will run day-to-day. Think about when you will be able to pay yourself, and any other people, and how much you will be able pay yourself/them. You may not always be able to rely on friends and volunteers to get things done.

CHAPTER 6

Paperwork Part 1: finance

Many growers and gardeners (in fact many people of any profession) have a mental block when it comes to paperwork – and if you mention Her Majesty's Revenue & Customs, a strange glazed look can come into their eyes. However, as with many irrational fears, when you actually start tackling paperwork it's never as bad as you thought. The key to paperwork is little and often: if you can keep on top of recording your sales and expenses as you go along, perhaps every weekend or at the end of every month, then you'll find that the rest of the papery pile pretty much does itself. If you struggle, there are various business and accounting courses you can go on; HMRC also offers free face-to-face courses around the country, to help with particular issues, such as Real Time Information PAYE – sign up for their newsletter to be kept informed. Or you can of course simply employ an accountant or bookkeeper to help you keep on top of the financial side of things. For any legal considerations, it would also make sense to pay a solicitor or legal adviser, for example to read through any tenancy contracts or give advice on any dispute or other legal matters. Some charities, such as the Prince's Trust, have a legal team who can help those eligible for their schemes; and the Federation of Small Businesses (FSB) can help with free legal and other advice to members (and also offers small businesses representation in the wider world).

Business structure

When setting up any new business, you need to decide on its legal structure, which determines your responsibilities with regard to paperwork, taxes and legal obligations. The four most common structures in commercial horticulture are sole trader, limited company, business partnership, and charity or not-for-profit community enterprise or group. Setting up as a sole trader is pretty straightforward, but for other legal structures it's definitely worth seeking legal advice to make sure that you choose the structure most appropriate for your business, and that you don't miss out important formalities.

Sole trader

This is the most basic and probably the easiest structure, at least to start with: you're a sole trader if you run your own business as an individual and you keep all the business profits after tax. You can still take on employees as a sole trader, but legally you are the only person responsible for the business and for any losses it makes. Any bills will be chargeable to you, and you'll be responsible for record keeping too. In order to set up as a sole trader, register with HMRC as soon as you can (and definitely within six months of starting up).

You'll have to fill in a Self Assessment tax return each tax year (issued in April; completion and payment deadline the end of the following January). It's very quick and easy to register online, or over the phone. Once filled in, the online form will automatically work out any National Insurance and income tax due. If your turnover is more than £79,000 per year (as of 2013-2014 – the registration threshold is updated every year, so double-check), you'll have to register for VAT too (see page 93). Don't forget that if the new business isn't your only source of income (for example, if you have another part-time job, or taxable savings), you'll also need to declare these on your tax return.

The other legal requirement relates to the business name: you can use your own name for this, or trade under a business name. If you choose a business name, you can't use offensive words, or use 'Limited', 'Ltd', 'public limited company', 'plc', 'limited liability partnership', 'LLP' or Welsh equivalents; nor can you "use sensitive words or expressions unless you have permission" (refer to Companies House for a list of these words), imply a connection with government or local authorities, or use a name that is too similar to a registered trademark or an existing business in the same sector (refer to Companies House for registered business names). You must include both your own name and business name (if different) on invoices and other paperwork.

Limited company

A limited company can be set up to run a business. The company's finances are separate from your own personal finances, and the company is entirely responsible for its actions. Any profits are owned by the company rather than by yourself; the company then shares out the money left after corporation tax is deducted to any members who own shares in the company. The company needs at least one director, who doesn't necessarily have to be a shareholder; and the company needs to be registered (incorporated) with Companies House, which confirms that the company legally exists.

While sole traders are personally responsible for business debts, the liability in a private company is usually limited to the shareholders. A private company 'limited by shares' has a 'share capital' (the money invested by the shareholders), and the liability of each member to any creditors is limited to the amount, if any, unpaid on their shares. This means that liability is limited to the value of the shares and any premium paid in return for the issue of the shares by the company. 'Limited by guarantee' means that the members will back the company up to a specific amount of money if necessary. This kind of company does not have a share capital and its members are guarantors rather than shareholders, so, unless they are shareholders too, they won't get any dividends from the company's profits. Unlike public limited companies, private companies cannot sell any shares to the general public. However, private companies' disclosure requirements are lighter than those of public limited companies.

A community interest company (CIC) is similar to the companies described above, but exists to benefit the community rather than individual shareholders. When applying to Companies House, you'll need to include a 'community interest statement' showing what your business plans to do, and make an 'asset lock', which promises that the company's assets will be used only for its social objectives, with limits on the money paid to shareholders. CIC applications will also automatically be sent to the Community Interest Companies Regulator. Some charities setting up this structure will also need to register with the Charity Commission.

When registering your limited company, you'll need 'articles of association': rules about running the company that everyone agrees to. Standard versions and templates of these articles are available to download from government websites.

Directors must try to make the company a success; follow the company's rules; make decisions for the benefit of the company; tell other shareholders if you personally might benefit from a transaction; keep good accounts and records; report changes to Companies House and HMRC; register for Self Assessment and send a personal Self Assessment tax return every year. Accountants or secretaries can look after some aspects of record keeping and accounting, but the director(s) is/are still legally responsible for them, and can be personally liable for losses or prosecuted if the rules are not followed.

Business partnership

An ordinary business partnership is between you and another partner or partners. Legal responsibilities, losses and profits are personally shared between the partners. Partners can also be legal entities, such as limited companies, rather than actual people. To set up a partnership, one partner must be chosen as the 'nominated partner' to register the partnership with HMRC (this automatically registers them for Self Assessment too); they will then be responsible for keeping records and doing partnership tax returns. Other partners must also register with HMRC for Self Assessment and do their own tax returns every year.

Limited partnerships are very similar, but limited partners are not personally liable for any losses or unpaid debts; these would be limited to the amount originally invested by each partner.

Not-for-profit group

There are several ways of setting up a 'not-for-profit group', which is run as a business, but one that reinvests any profits after expenses are paid. These groups can include community or social enterprises, which use trade to earn money which is then ploughed back into the business. It's possible for a community group to become an unincorporated association, which is free to set up, but this is not a legal structure so is not recognised by law. Individual members of an unincorporated association are personally responsible for any debts or agreements. The governing document is a constitution or set of rules, and there is usually a membership and a management committee. Such not-for-profit unincorporated groups are pretty casual and, while not legally charities, are usually charitable in spirit. Some might become trusts: a more formal legal arrangement for not-for-profit groups whereby one or more 'trustees' are made legally responsible for holding assets such as land or money for the benefit of one or more 'beneficiaries' – which could be the whole community who want good food. Trusts have no protection from liability for the trustees, however. As an alternative to the more unofficial options described above, charities can set up as a charitable incorporated organisation (CIO), which is a legal structure. Information must be sent to the Charity Commission electronically. You'll need to choose and complete one of the model constitutions, and apply online. The governing document will be a constitution, and the trustees will be protected in most circumstances against contractual liabilities.

A number of structures are possible if starting up a co-operative, depending on the number of members and whether it intends to make profit for members or not: your choice will depend on your members and how you plan on running the business. There is plenty of advice available for those considering setting up a co-operative; part of the ethos of running a co-operative is helping others do the same. Taking specialist legal advice in the early stages is recommended.

Financial responsibilities

Once you have decided on which type of legal structure will best suit you and your business, you'll need to work out what your financial obligations are – especially for The Taxman. Don't be scared: these matters are pretty straightforward, and once you get on top of them it should be fairly easy to keep up.

Registering for VAT

Most businesses that make 'taxable supplies' of over £79,000 in 12 months will need to register for Value Added Tax (VAT) (check the latest registration threshold). This means that you will need to add VAT to any goods or services you provide, unless they are VAT-exempt. The three levels of VAT charges are currently 0 per cent (zero rate), 5 per cent (reduced rate) and 20 per cent (standard rate) on top of the value of your goods or services. Most food and drink for human consumption, especially basic ingredients such as vegetables and fruit, are zero-rated, which means that there are no extra charges to add to the veg you sell, even if you are registered for VAT. The benefit is that, once you are registered for VAT, you can claim back any VAT that you have paid on goods and services coming into the business. In particular, when buying new equipment this can save you hundreds or even thousands of pounds.

If you sell any flowers, ornamental vegetables, compost or 'added value' products such as fruit juices or young plants not for human consumption, and you're registered for VAT, you will need to add the relevant VAT charge to your goods (usually the standard rate of 20 per cent) and produce a VAT invoice for your customers. This is quite simple, though, once you have a template: you just need to clearly show what the original price is, what the VAT chargeable is, what the total price including VAT is, and your VAT registration number and details.

It is possible to voluntarily register for VAT, even if you haven't sold over £79,000 of taxable goods in 12 months, in order to take advantage of VAT rebates. You can also backdate your voluntary registration by up to four years, so it's possible to claim back VAT on purchases you have already made, as long as you have the right evidence. The only downside to registering for VAT for a market garden is filling in a VAT return form every three months. However, this is a very simple form that you can complete online, and should only take a couple of minutes, providing you have kept good records of all incoming purchases and any VAT receipts, and sales records, with any VAT chargeable on your goods.

HMRC has a number of comprehensive guides online to explain whether you should register for VAT, how to calculate your VAT turnover, which goods are exempt from VAT, and what the VAT rates for all goods are. If in doubt, give HMRC a ring.

Opening a bank account

If you're a sole trader, it is possible to have all payments and debits going into and out of your own personal bank account. However, if you are getting a business loan or grant as part of your funding, one of the conditions of the loan or grant might be that you have a separate business account. A dedicated account in your business name also looks more professional, and it is easier to keep track of exactly what you have spent on the business, and who has paid you.

Most banks and building societies do charge for 'maintaining' business accounts, even if there are very few payments in and out of it. Some will charge a flat monthly rate, which might cover a few online payments and a limited number of cheque or cash payments or debits, with extra charges for activity over the limited level, as well as for going overdrawn, payments being refused and so on. Compare business accounts carefully, and choose one that will best suit your method of payments and debits. For instance, if you're going to take most of your payments in cash on a market stall, and you don't want to keep the money in your house, you'll want to bank it without getting penalised too much for making cash payments into your account. Likewise, if you're planning on asking your veg box or wholesale customers to pay you online weekly, you'll want an account that allows you to have a large number of small incoming payments, without charging you 30p a time on payments of £5, for example.

You might find some banks or building societies that offer free business banking accounts, but this is usually for accounts managed solely online, so you'll find it hard to actually talk to someone about any queries. The Federation of Small Businesses (FSB) also offers free banking with the Co-operative Bank, so if you're a member you can get a good deal. If you're not already a member, consider whether the joining fee is worth free banking and the other FSB member benefits on offer.

Simple accounts

It's worth getting into the habit of noting down all your invoices, takings and expenses every week – with one page for income and another for expenses. You could also highlight any invoices not yet paid, and tick off those that have been paid, so you can keep an eye on any outstanding payments and send out reminders. Some cash books and accounting software also allow you to include more detailed information, such as the method of payment (cash, cheque, online and so on), which can be useful when dealing with a large number of different customers and payments.

Spreadsheets come into their own here, and are deceptively simple. Excel or the equivalent are surprisingly powerful programmes (and open-source software such as Open Office is also free to download): you can use them for making easily updateable price lists, digital 'cash books', invoices, expenses and other accounting documents. There are also a lot of other accounting software packages, such as Sage, of varying price and sophistication. All of this record keeping can be done on paper the old-fashioned way, of course, but simple spreadsheets make editing them much easier, and it's also easy to cross-reference, for example invoices with your income in your cash book, if they are all spreadsheets.

When it comes to paperwork, spreadsheets are your friend. The automatic calculations will help you to see if you're taking enough money in relation to your expenses, who your best customers are, and where you biggest costs are. Your accounts will thereby help you determine whether the business is sustainable, to look at ways of cutting costs if necessary or focusing on certain types of customer, and to put together projections for the following year.

Example cash book: money in

Date	Invoice	Total amount (inc. VAT)
1/10/13	Helpful Hotel, invoice ref HH001	£100
2/10/13	Market stall takings	£200
2/10/13	Fabulous Farm Shop & Florists, invoice ref FF001	£55
4/10/13	Helpful Hotel, invoice ref HH002	£120
5/10/13	Veg box Mr Jones	£10
6/10/13	Promising Primary School, invoice ref PP001	£100

Example cash book: money out

Date	Description	Total amount	VAT	Equipment (less VAT)
1/10/13	Seeds, Pukka Seed Co.	£400	£0	
2/10/13	Polytunnel, Tasty Tunnels Ltd	£1,200	£200	£1,000
4/10/13	Leaflets, Professional Marketing Co.	£30	£5	
5/10/13	Rent, Farmer Giles	£250	£0	
6/10/13	Insurance, Friends Mutual Ltd	£350	£0	
8/10/13	Phone bill, Green Telecom	£30	£5	

VAT	Wholesale takings (less VAT)	Direct takings (less VAT)	Paid	Rent (less VAT)	Seeds & compost (less VAT)	Insurance (less VAT)	Stationery & marketing (less VAT)	Other (less VAT)
£0	£100	£0	✔		£400			
£0	£0	£200	✔					
£5	£50	£0	✔				£25	
£0	£120	£0		£250				
£0	£0	£10	✔			£350		
£0	£100	£0						£25

Invoices and payment methods

Some customers won't need to be invoiced of course, such as those from a market stall or other immediate cash sales (although you will need to keep a record for your accounts of how much money you have taken in total); but for many types of sale you will need to issue some sort of invoice or receipt. You may like to use a simple carbon-copy duplicate invoice book, especially if you're being paid cash or cheque on delivery.

Most larger wholesale customers, however, won't pay by any method on delivery, but rather will wait for at least a week after delivery; some may not pay until after a month or two, and will want more official invoices with your payment details on them, so they can either send you a cheque, pay by card over the phone (if you have a card machine), or pay directly into your bank. Card readers are becoming more readily available and affordable to run, so could be useful for immediate payments and to keep the cash flow going – they can be used not only for payments by phone but also at your market stall or your premises, if you have a shop or other outlet. Some banks can offer card readers as part of your account package, or there are independent companies who will provide you with a phone line and card machine to use; they then claim a percentage of your takings, and/or charge you a monthly usage fee before paying you the net amount for that week or month.

Find out what your bank will charge you for cash, cheque, card or online payments, and try to encourage your customers to pay via the more economical method (probably online payments). It's also worth working out whether you'd rather have small, regular payments to ease cash flow (but be charged each time you pay in an amount), or a lump sum every month or so to reduce bank charges, but which will hold up cash flow. Then send invoices accordingly, with your payment terms.

Invoices should be dated and show every item being charged, with a unit or weight price, and subtotals. Include any VAT if you are registered and including a VAT chargeable item. Include an invoice number too for reference, your bank details, postal address, and other contact details.

Finance checklist

- Consider the options for a legal structure. Which would suit your business best? Being a sole trader is the quickest to set up, and has the least amount of paperwork involved, but you will personally be liable for any losses. Members of a limited company will be liable only up to the amount they originally invested, but there is a little more paperwork involved each year.

- Think about whether you want to keep any profit, or just earn a wage from your business. If you are only after a wage, you could consider a not-for-profit or charitable approach, and invest any profits back into the business.

- Take legal advice when setting up your legal structure, or at least advice from someone who has set up a similar enterprise and can guide you through the processes.

- Register with HMRC for Self Assessment, VAT if applicable, and any other tax returns relevant to your business.

- Choose a bank account: compare interest rates, account maintenance and other charges, and any benefits such the as use of a card machine, if relevant to your business.

- Familiarise yourself with simple spreadsheets, if you haven't already: they will help with invoicing and your end-of-year tax returns, and keep track of your cash flow.

CHAPTER 7

Paperwork Part 2: law and orders

Apart from the accounting, the other main aspect of running a business that might put some people off is the legal side of things: dealing with contracts, making sure you have the right insurance and that you're not breaking the law when selling your veg and so on. However, most of these factors are pure common sense – and there are plenty of professional grower and smallholder bodies, such as the National Farmers' Union (NFU) and Organic Growers Alliance (OGA), who will be happy to offer advice and point you in the right direction for guidance. You can also get legal advice via charities or the Citizens Advice Bureau or from the Federation of Small Businesses (FSB).

Contracts and leases

Unless you own your land, you'll need to arrange some kind of contract with your landlord, or a suitable agreement if you own the land as part of a group or co-operative. Depending on your particular set-up, there are various templates that comply with the Agricultural Tenancies Act that can be used and adapted to suit your circumstances (these are available to buy online, or via a solicitor), so you won't have to draw up a legal document from scratch. If you're renting from a farmer, the chances are that they will already have a basic template that can just be adapted to suit you. Get some legal advice at this stage to help clarify anything unclear or ambiguous in your contract. If you're setting up a CSA scheme, it's a great help if someone on the committee or board of directors or trustees has some knowledge of legal matters. Legal aid is available to those earning under £20,000 per year, but services are usually only available for 'dispute issues', so may not be available for your business queries; check with a local legal adviser. Some law practices offer free short 'taster' time slots to give advice on legal matters such as contracts.

Some land-use contracts are quite short term, at least when you start out, because both tenant and landlord may be quite hesitant about committing long term to a new venture. However, provided there is a good notice period on either side (so if your landlord wants you to leave or sells the land, you have to be told in good time, ideally a year in advance or more), there's nothing wrong with a rolling yearly or five-yearly contract. Once you've been going for a year or two and both sides have got to know each other (and the nature of the business) better, you could negotiate a longer tenancy for added security. Your notice period and contract length will depend to some extent on what you plan to grow and your business model: if you're growing fruit trees or perennials, you'll probably want more security than if you are just growing annuals each year. Some landlords might see inheriting a load of fruit trees from the deal as a bonus; others might insist that any trees be removed before you vacate the plot – so find out the position as soon as possible, and meet to discuss your respective plans for the site.

Ensure that your contract also specifies who owns what: for instance, if you have bought any polytunnels, sheds or packhouses, you'll need to make sure that's clearly in the contract as belonging to you; and if any benefactor donates something like a greenhouse to you, get that noted at the earliest opportunity too, just so there's no misunderstanding. Although it might seem a bit embarrassing to chase a busy landlord or benefactor for a contract and signature, it's worth it to prevent awkwardness – or worse – in the future.

Most contracts should cover the following: who the tenant and landlord are, where and what the holding is (this could include a map), what the rent is and when it's payable; the letting clause (why the tenant is using the land, what the business is); the tenant's obligations (check these carefully); the landlord's obligations; termination of contract clauses and notice periods; any break clauses (for example, death or illness); how to resolve disputes. Add anything else you would like to be made clear too, such as a list of who owns what if there is a group of people involved, to prevent lapses of memory in the future.

Allotment restrictions

Allotment holders are generally permitted to sell any surplus produce, but if the allotment is owned by the council, this will depend on the particular local authority and its lease agreement. Some allotment societies have an unwritten rule that produce is not allowed to be sold but can be bartered or swapped, and produce can be 'sold' by a number of plot-holders for charity – where technically it is given away, and suggested donations are made at the same time for raising funds.

There is also an ethical point to consider here, and a question of how 'surplus produce' is defined. It can seem pretty unfair if there is a long waiting list for an allotment on a site, and one allotment holder is growing so much veg that they are able to sell most or all of it. Most private allotments don't have any legal restrictions on them, but check your agreement with your landlord, in case there are any caveats prohibiting selling produce from the farm gate (especially if the landlord has a shop next door). If selling is allowed, consider teaming up with other like-minded plot-holders to form a mini co-operative, in order to supply more variety and quantity.

Planning permission

If you're planning to build any large structures such as barns or packhouses near your market garden, you'll have to check whether you need to apply for planning permission from your local council, and put in any application as soon as possible, because it can take some time to complete this process. Different councils have different requirements, and different levels of efficiency at processing applications – and will charge you different amounts too.

Generally speaking, outbuildings such as sheds and polytunnels under 3m high tend to come under the 'permitted development' umbrella, which means that you don't need to apply for planning permission provided that any applicable limits or area restrictions are met. This can depend on the exact nature of the structure, exactly where your plot is (if it's on designated land in an Area of Outstanding Natural Beauty, for instance, then there are likely to be complaints if you install a fleet of polytunnels in a sensitive spot), and on the local authority. If you're in any doubt, it's worth approaching your Local Planning Authority (LPA) sooner rather than later, to check whether you do need permission. Many councils have an environmental and local food policy, so will hopefully look favourably on your project and plans and will process your query and any subsequent application quickly. Plus, if you let them know your plans, they may even be a source of future customers or volunteers, or a drop-off point for veg boxes.

With all building work, the owner of the property or land is ultimately responsible for complying with the relevant planning rules and Building Regulations, so you will need to work with the landowner when applying for any planning permission. If you discover after the structure has been built that you don't have the correct planning permission from your local authority, it is still possible to apply for retrospective permission, but the building will have to meet all the usual requirements, and any restrictions in the area will still apply.

Insurance

As a business, you'll need insurance to cover any unforeseen incidents, as well as to give you peace of mind. You'll need public liability insurance if members of the public will have access to your premises, such as when buying their veg, which will cover any accidents that happen there. Public liability is usually the standard starting point on a business insurance policy.

You'll also need product liability insurance, to cover the produce that you're selling. While fresh ingredients have very few risks associated with them, I think it's always best to be over-cautious in this sort of area: what happens if someone turns out to be allergic to something in your salad bags? Or cracks a tooth on a particularly hard carrot? While common sense should cover most incidents that might potentially arise, insurance will cover any legal costs incurred as a result of someone taking you to court (definitely a worst-case scenario). My public and product liability insurance, for my 2-acre garden, is around £260 per year. Insurance companies use different factors when calculating premiums, including the size of the land and business, any equipment, the location, and what you'll be growing or rearing.

You will need to add employer's insurance if you take on extra help. This is compulsory, even if you don't pay your workers (i.e. if they are volunteers), although there are exemptions, for instance family businesses where all employees are close family members. It will cost from around £350 per year for a 2-acre garden using a couple of seasonal workers; premiums will depend on your annual payroll and on the nature of the work. Employer's Insurance covers any injury sustained by your volunteers or employees, as well as any compensation claims at a future date.

Other insurance extras to consider are cover for any outbuildings or polytunnels (specialist insurers offer this), against damage caused by flooding, snow or fire. You can also insure valuable tools and equipment against damage or theft. If you have a van or car used just for business, that will also need insurance of course; if you use your own car for business purposes, don't forget to make sure your insurance policy covers you for business use (you can also claim tax back for any mileage done in the name of the business). You might also want to insure against loss of revenue or earnings (so you'd be covered if the weather ruins everything, like in 2012), and also personal injury cover, in case an injury renders you unable to work.

Insurance is available from a number of providers, although it's worth talking to NFU Mutual, since agricultural businesses are their speciality, so they are likely to understand your business better than some larger remote banks or insurance providers. In general, special deals may be available if you hold home insurance with the same company.

Staff and employees

If you decide that you're not able to manage on your own, you'll need to get some help in – paid or otherwise. Depending on the size of your holding and the nature of the produce you're growing, you might prefer to rely on volunteers and WWOOFers, who can work in exchange for food and usually lodging or a place to camp. Many growers use casual seasonal labour; if people work for you on a freelance, self-employed basis for a few weeks, they will just need to invoice you for their wages rather than be on your payroll, so you can keep your accounts in order (in practice, it may be you who writes up the invoices). As long as you have employer's insurance and a Health and Safety policy (see opposite) in place, it's pretty straightforward.

However, you might decide that you have enough work year-round to take on someone full- or part-time. It'll help to produce a job description and advertise the job locally, through word of mouth, local papers or shop windows, or try the Organic Growers Alliance (OGA); you could also consider taking on an apprentice or seasonal worker via the Soil Association's Future Growers Scheme (they will advertise the vacancy for you). You should have a clear idea of exactly what the job will entail and how much you'll pay per hour (check the latest minimum wage information with HMRC) – taking into account the extra costs to you such as employer's National Insurance (if applicable; tax relief on employers' contributions up to £2,000 is available for small businesses from April 2014) and extra administrative work. It's essential to register as an employer with HMRC and set up your payroll processes – and you'll need to fill in employer's tax returns. You will also need to provide a workplace pension too.

If you have five or more workers, you'll also need to have a Health and Safety policy in place and written down (check the Health and Safety Executive's website for the latest guidance). Fewer than five people, and you just need to have a policy that everyone knows – but that can be based on common-sense awareness of potential risks, such as ladders, tools lying around, water and electricity, and so on. Horticulture is generally a low-risk business, so just be sensible and encourage anyone working for you not to put a fork through their foot, fall off ladders or place their hands in the wood-chipper, and to look out for any devious rakes lying hidden in the grass.

Each employee is legally entitled to a written pay statement (weekly or monthly), as well as written details of the terms and conditions of their employment (a contract) within two months of their starting work. Basic templates for these are available to buy online, although it is worth seeking professional advice and getting contracts tailor-made to prevent misunderstandings.

Employees are entitled to statutory sick pay, statutory maternity pay, and statutory paid holiday entitlement. Paid holiday leave is the equivalent of 5.6 weeks of their regular working week (so if, for example, they are part-time and work two days a week, it is the equivalent of 5.6 weeks of their part-time hours, which is 11.2 days per year). Statutory paid holiday entitlement is limited to 28 days per year, and employers can choose to include bank holidays and public holidays as part of the statutory paid holiday.

Environmental health

You are required by law to register any premises used to prepare, store, transport or sell food with your local authority's Environmental Health Department a month before any premises open; the frequency of their visits will depend on the type of business. However, since horticulture doesn't involve processing food but simply supplying raw vegetative ingredients, it is seen as a very low-risk business. Registering just involves filling out a free, simple, one-off form, which the council keeps on file; you need to notify the council only if there's a change of business operator, if you move or if the nature of the business changes.

Although there are few environmental health considerations in a market garden business, it's sensible to
take usual common-sense precautions, especially
when selling fresh leafy veg such as salads: wash your
hands before picking, use mains or filtered water for
irrigation to prevent contaminated matter leaving a
residue on leaves (if reusing rainwater or fresh water,
you'll need a special filter to prevent bacteria build-
up), don't use fresh manure as compost (especially if
a salad crop is to follow), wash out thoroughly any
reused picking containers and so on. It's also worth
including a note on labels on any fresh leafy produce
suggesting that customers wash the produce before
consuming.

Labelling and trades descriptions

Trading standards issues such as mislabelling of food
products or misdescribing businesses are handled by
local authorities. With regard to labelling, two main
requirements arise in practice for vegetable growers:
packaging and invoicing should be accurate, and all
claims should be true. So, for example, if you sell and
invoice for two kilos of carrots, you'll need to make
sure that you have accurate scales and are not short-
changing your customers. Scales can be tested if
you're unsure of their accuracy (contact your local
trading standards for a test, which costs from around
£10), or you could just double-check by weighing on
another pair of scales. All descriptions of your produce
should be accurate too, though this is not a common
problem for market gardeners, whose produce is visible

for all to see (it's not easy to pass off fresh carrots as tomatoes, unlike horse meat and beef in processed food).

The requirement for accurate description also applies to the business and how the produce is grown. You may consider yourself as an eco-friendly organic grower and business, and therefore your produce as organic – but unless you are certified by an official organic certification body such as the Soil Association or Organic Farmers & Growers (OF&G), you are not allowed by law to describe your produce as 'organic' – this word is protected by European Law. If you choose to be certified, you will need to adhere to the body's organic standards, you'll be inspected at least every year, and you'll be expected to keep detailed records of your growing methods, rotation plans and compost applications and other external inputs, along with other documents such as the details and organic certificates of suppliers of any bought-in produce. You'll also need to go into a 'conversion period' for two years while converting to organic growing (unless the land you are growing on is already certified as organic): during this time you cannot describe your produce as organic, but you can say it is 'in-conversion' produce.

Annual organic certification fees start from around £360 (plus VAT) – usually a bit cheaper while you're in conversion – and depend on the size of the holding.

Some market gardeners, especially those on smaller holdings, choose not to certify their business to start with (mostly because of the cost), and rely on showing their customers exactly how they grow. The Wholesome Food Association is an unofficial collection of like-minded food producers who promise to grow and farm in an organic way, and have an open-gate policy, allowing their premises to be inspected or visited at any time. However, in practice this association is not very active and it is less well-known than organic certifying bodies, but at least membership shows the values you hold, and when you join (costing around £27 per year) you can use their logo on your produce, and get listed on their website.

Legal checklist

- Look into the options for obtaining legal advice: if you can't afford to pay a solicitor, find out if legal aid may be available, or if any of your funding sources (e.g. community or charity) could provide legal guidance themselves or extra funding for a solicitor.

- Finalise any contracts (such as business tenancy agreements and employees' terms and conditions) with the help of your legal representative.

- Work out whether you need planning permission for any polytunnels or outbuildings, and apply for permission as soon as possible. If you don't own the land, you'll need to do this with the landowner.

- Decide whether you need any other insurance on top of public and product liability: e.g. employer's insurance; personal injury insurance for yourself; insurance to cover loss, theft or damage to any expensive equipment.

- Will you be employing more than five people? Then you'll need to write down your Health and Safety policy.

- Think about whether you will put your workers on the payroll, or will only employ seasonal casual labour. Register with your local council's Environmental Health Department at the council.

- Ensure that your produce descriptions are accurate. Will you go down the certified organic route?

CHAPTER 8

What to grow

A market garden is a constant juggling act: a matter of trying to keep a range of different crops happy in the same space, and trying to make sure every inch of ground is productive for as long as possible. It's easy to ignore the organic principle of using green manures to include a 'rest' or ley period in your rotation: that's valuable cropping space out of production! But leaving a patch down to a leguminous fertility-building mixture for a year or so will honestly pay you back in the future: with fewer weed, pest and disease problems, soil that is better able to adapt to adverse weather conditions, and improved yields. If you allow your green manures to flower (but not set seed), it will not only look pretty but you'll also attract a vast amount of wildlife – and that's a great advert for your business too.

Crop rotations can seem very awkward when it comes to trying to make a patch profitable (brassicas are usually the culprits when a rotation breaks down, because they are easy to grow, include a huge number of crops, mostly fetch a decent price, and take up a lot of space), but actually establishing a good rotation can be very positive. A rotation makes you grow a variety of crops from different families, which means that you'll pretty much always have a range on offer for sale (apart from in the 'hungry gap' of March/April to July, perhaps). It also means that you won't have all your eggs in one basket, in case pest, disease or bad weather strikes one particular crop. In 2011, my carrots were amazing, but leeks were small and disappointing; the following very wet year, slugs had every single carrot but I had a bumper leek crop. This mixture of swings and roundabouts means that at least I always had *something* to sell; if I had been growing only carrots or leeks over the two years, I wouldn't have had a crop at all for a year.

A five-year rotation is common in market gardens. So, your patch could be divided into five roughly equal sections: green manures; brassicas; umbellifers such as carrots and parsnips; alliums such as leeks and spring onions with legumes such as beans and peas;

and others such as beetroot, spinach, squashes, courgettes and lettuce.

Profitable produce

There is a huge range of books dedicated to growing vegetables, herbs, fruit and flowers, and they all look gorgeous – but it can be difficult trying to work out what is actually profitable to grow. It's all too easy to just grow what you enjoy growing (I love growing chillies) and what is easy to grow (potatoes are pretty foolproof), rather than what sells – these are not necessarily the same thing. If you stick with crops that are easy to grow, you might face problems when it comes to selling produce that most gardeners and allotmenteers in the area have also grown, for the same reasons. If a particular crop is abundant locally, that will also tend to be reflected in the (lower) price you'll get for it. Your passion for certain plants may not be reflected in the local population either: I can sell perhaps a kilo of chillies a year, but each chilli plant can produce up to 100 chillies, so I end up drying most and using them myself.

On the other hand, if you are growing on a new site, it can be quite sensible to grow 'easy' crops that are pretty tolerant and unfussy for the first year at least: simple brassicas such as autumn cabbage, kale and purple sprouting broccoli; the usual roots (carrots and parsnips); beetroot, chard and lettuce; perhaps some peas, and broad or runner beans. Then you will at least have time to see what your new land is like –

whether there are unproductive patches, bits that stay very wet or dry all year, or areas that will benefit from a few years' resting, green manure or other treatment. If you are on a new site, it's also worth growing a few different varieties of each crop if possible, to see which ones do well in your soil and microclimate.

You might decide that 'everyday' crops such as green cabbage, maincrop potatoes and yellow onions simply don't make enough of a return to justify growing them – especially if you're limited for space. As a rule, salad items and more unusual crops tend to fetch the highest price, although in any given year particular national or regional problems such as weather or blight might mean that traditional low-value crops can be sold at a premium. If you have a very small space in which to grow, you may decide to specialise in something like salad leaves, 'baby' crops such as leeks, carrots or parsnips – pulled when young to maximise space – or really specialist items such as unusually coloured vegetables or hard-to-find veg grown for a particular market, such as Asian or African food stores and restaurants.

Your market research (see Chapter 3) should already have given you an idea of the kind of crops that are in demand in your area. Fresh leafy items such as mixed salad leaves always seem to be in demand whatever the region – probably because these kinds of crop don't keep for very long, so are best not bought from huge wholesalers and transported around the country. Customers can see straight away whether a bag of salad leaves has been picked recently or not. Lettuce and many other salad leaf seeds are relatively cheap and the plants easy to grow; they don't take up too much time in the ground either, so the same patch can be reused for something else before and after the crop, making salads better value to grow per square metre over the whole growing season.

It's also worth bearing in mind that profitable crops are not necessarily the same as valuable crops. For instance, asparagus is often seen as an expensive crop, but that's partly because the costs of production are high: the cropping window for asparagus is only a few weeks, and it takes a few years of establishing the crop before you can take any decent yield from the crowns; plus they need plenty of room. Sometimes your most profitable crop might be a relative cheap-to-buy vegetable, simply because the costs of production are low.

Your own production costs will depend on your set-up, what you grow and how you grow it. I now create spreadsheets of those of my crops that I think are the most profitable, crunch the figures using the calculations shown on the next two pages, and work out how much (very roughly) each crop makes per pound spent on it. The results can be quite surprising! It's worth bearing in mind, however, that some of these crops might be at their limit of profitability and can't be scaled up or down very much: for instance, if I decided to grow more nasturtiums, I might find that there isn't a market for any extra nasturtium sales other than those I've already made, so the extra crop would go to waste. Likewise, if I didn't grow many tomatoes and therefore had only a very limited supply, then some of my chef customers and other outlets might choose to go elsewhere for all their tomatoes, since my supply could be erratic and not enough for their needs, so I might not sell many at all.

Crop costings

The cost of growing any crop broadly comprises the costs of the seed, equipment and so on, and the fixed costs of the space it takes up while it is growing.

Fixed costs

The following illustration shows how I calculated roughly how much a square metre of my land costs for any given crop – in the polytunnels, in the larger field, or in the exposed herb beds between the polytunnels.

The cost of the polytunnels themselves was around £1,800 (not including the plastic cladding); covering 815m², which makes £2.21/m². If the structure lasts 20 years, this works out as £0.11/m²/year.

The tunnel plastic, covering the same area, does not last so long – perhaps five years. It costs £634: so works out as £0.78/m², and £0.16/m²/year over five years.

Lastly the tunnel irrigation, Mypex ground-cover fabric, cucumber netting and other fixings cost in total approximately £540 and again could last for five years, over the same area: so £0.66/m², and £0.13/m²/year.

The field and herb beds' irrigation, nets and other bits and pieces, all lasting at least five years, cost around £400, and cover the field of 11,840m². This makes £0.03/m², and £0.007/m²/year over five years.

The total rent for the whole site (£12,655m²) is £250/year, which is £0.02/m²/year, for both tunnels and field.

So the total fixed costs for a square metre of space in the field or herb beds is £0.007 + £0.02, which is approximately £0.03/m²/year.

The total fixed costs for a square metre of polytunnel space is £0.11 + £0.16 + £0.13 + £0.02, which makes £0.42/m²/year.

Individual costs for each crop

The tables on the following pages show my costings for those crops that I thought might be most profitable, and the sales return made on them. I had quite a good idea of roughly what each crop cost me, but it was interesting to see how much more expensive protected crops are. Because of this, crops grown out in the field became more profitable; although chard was grown outside in the summer, and indoors over winter.

Crop costs

Crop	Seed cost total	Compost, heat, trays & pots costs total	Sowing, planting & weeding costs total	Harvest costs total	Growing space – indoor (m²)
Aubergines	£4.60	£2.00	£4.00	£3.50	25
Basil	£13.00	£4.00	£4.00	£3.50	30
Beetroot	£23.80	£0.00	£7.00	£14.00	76
Calabrese	£10.05	£3.00	£4.00	£7.00	
Carrots	£33.45	£0.00	£14.00	£21.00	36
Chard	£8.60	£2.00	£7.00	£10.00	24
Cucumbers	£7.95	£5.00	£10.00	£7.00	37
French beans	£21.45	£0.00	£18.00	£21.00	
Garlic	£0.00	£0.00	£3.50	£7.00	
Herbs	£12.00	£6.00	£20.00	£14.00	
Kale	£14.65	£4.00	£10.00	£14.00	
Leeks	£25.50	£0.00	£35.00	£35.00	77
Lettuce	£14.35	£7.00	£20.00	£14.00	30
Micro leaves	£260.00	£100.00	£30.00	£14.00	
Nasturtiums	£3.00	£1.00	£8.00	£14.00	
Parsnips	£15.00	£0.00	£7.00	£14.00	
Peppers	£5.75	£4.00	£4.00	£3.50	45
Purple sprouting broccoli	£10.80	£3.00	£10.00	£21.00	
Salad bags	£30.00	£10.00	£30.00	£30.00	640
Spinach	£5.75	£0.00	£4.00	£3.00	30
Tomatoes	£25.25	£6.00	£130.00	£130.00	185
Total	£544.95	£157.00	£379.50	£400.50	

Notes

Not including cost of reusable seed & module tray

Includes time preparing ground, adding manures, planting, laying Mypex, side-shooting, thinning, staking & tying

Includes time washing & net-shifting; packaging costs (bags, punnets)

Time costs: £7/hour (own labour value – a pretty basic starting wage)

Time costs: £7/hour (own labour value)

Ground time – indoor (months)	Indoor cost total (space × £0.42 × proportion of year)	Growing space – outdoor (m²)	Ground time – outdoor (months)	Outdoor cost total (space × £0.03 × proportion of year)	Total cost per m² per year
6	£5.25				£19.35
3	£3.15				£27.65
8	£21.28	61	5	£0.76	£66.84
		120	7	£2.10	£26.15
6	£7.56	480	1	£1.20	£77.21
6	£5.04	90	9	£2.03	£34.67
6	£7.77				£37.72
		300	6	£4.50	£64.95
		30	10	£0.75	£11.25
		61	12	£1.83	£53.83
		250	11	£6.88	£49.53
3	£8.09	740	8	£14.80	£118.39
4	£4.20	240	7	£4.20	£63.75
					£404.00
		2	7	£0.04	£26.04
		280	3	£2.10	£38.10
6	£9.45				£26.70
		250	11	£6.88	£51.68
7	£156.80				£256.80
3	£3.15				£15.90
7	£45.32				£336.57
	£277.06			£48.07	£1,807.08

Not including propagating tunnel time

Includes successive sowings

Includes successive sowings

Crop profitability

Crop	Total cost	Total sold	Return per £1
Aubergines	£19.35	£13.16	£0.68
Basil	£27.65	£15.50	£0.56
Beetroot	£66.84	£149.40	£2.24
Calabrese	£26.15	£23.81	£0.91
Carrots	£77.21	£176.44	£2.29
Chard	£34.67	£214.20	£6.18
Cucumbers	£37.72	£131.65	£3.49
French beans	£64.95	£144.03	£2.22
Garlic	£11.25	£50.90	£4.52
Herbs	£53.83	£181.10	£3.36
Kale	£49.53	£281.20	£5.68
Leeks	£118.39	£673.43	£5.69
Lettuce	£63.75	£284.75	£4.47
Micro leaves	£404.00	£1,123.05	£2.78
Nasturtiums	£26.04	£67.00	£2.57
Parsnips	£38.10	£130.78	£3.43
Peppers	£26.70	£32.16	£1.20
Purple sprouting broccoli	£51.68	£132.28	£2.56
Salad bags	£256.80	£1,295.70	£5.05
Spinach	£15.90	£38.65	£2.43
Tomatoes	£336.57	£874.51	£2.60
			Average return/£1:
Total	£1,807.08	£6,033.70	£3.09
Notes		The outlined boxes show which crops raised the most money	The shaded boxes show the crops that made a loss (returned less than £1 for every £1 invested)
			The outlined boxes show which crops gave the best return (profit of 500-600% or more)

Comments

Poor yield again: seed/weather?

Some used in salad bags

Still cropping 2013

Slugs ate first sowing

No maincrop survived in field; only polytunnel bunches & 2011 remnants

Still cropping 2013: superstar!

Late planting

Slugs ate first sowing; third sowing frosted; good for wildlife (bumblebees)

Saved seed, grown through already-laid Mypex 2012

Some perennial seed cost spread over time; beneficial flowers (various pollinators); some leaves used in salad bags

Slugs killed early plants; still cropping 2013

Excellent yield 2013, in the most productive field patch

Some used in salad bags; still cropping 2013

Only grown in module trays in propagation tunnel, no cost per m²

Good for wildlife (bumblebees)

No 2012 crop (slugs); remnants of winter 2011 crop

Slugs ate early plants; second later planting successful

Most plants rotted in field winter 2013

Approximate seed cost; most popular crop

Slugs ate several sowings in tunnels & one in field (no surviving crop in field)

Good yield despite weather; high labour costs (fortnightly side-shooting)

How much to grow

You may now have decided which crops to grow, and perhaps have an idea of which varieties to trial, but then how much of each crop will you need? Again, this is something you'll need to establish during your market research: while chefs and other customers may ask for a specific crop, such as sweetcorn or butternut squash, they may not specify how much of each they would be likely to buy. You will most likely be bounded to some extent by your space and rotation limitations – but if you can work out roughly how much of each crop you'd like to grow, or need to grow, you can work backwards from there. For instance, if you know that you'll most likely sell just a few bags or punnets of herbs each year, and you only have room for a small herb bed, then you won't need to order more than a few small packets of herb seed. Of course it's always better to have too many plants coming on and ready to plant out than too few, in case of pest or disease attacks, plus you could always try selling surplus herb or vegetable plants, or swap them for something useful from a neighbour.

Working out how much of each crop you need is something best learned from experience, and trial and error; but as a starting point, try filling in the useful horticultural cropping tool shown on the following pages, developed by Ben Raskin for the Soil Association's CSA scheme. It is free to download from the Soil Association's website, and can be adjusted and modified to fit your plans. Simply enter how many people you'd like to feed (it is currently aimed at box schemes, but would also work for other market outlets), and change the yield prediction depending on how optimistic and confident you're feeling. Then the calculator works out the total area you need to sow or plant for each crop.

What to grow checklist

- Do you know which crops are in demand in your area? Check your market research to see what kinds of things are hard to get hold of but are still desirable. Fresh leaves, such as salads and spinach, are usually a good start, and are mostly easy to grow in many soil types too.

- Find a good balance of crops that you will feel confident growing, will do well in your conditions, and which you think will be in demand.

- Don't forget that crop rotations and including green manures in the planting cycle are not stopping you from making money: you're investing in the soil, to decrease your weed burden and improve the soil structure and fertility for future seasons, and you're also spreading the risk in case some crops fail.

- Use the horticultural tool to work out roughly how much of each crop you'll need; work out your costs of production, and what your profit margin might be on each – is this enough? Try out some valuable crop combinations to suit your location, circumstances and market.

Horticultural cropping tool

| No of people per year | 100 | Yield prediction | high |

Crop	Quantity per person per week	No. of people per year	No. of weeks supply per year	Total quantity per year	Price per unit
Onions (kg)	0.5	100	52	2600	£1.40
Red onions (kg)	0.5	100	20	1000	£1.50
Leeks (kg)	0.3	100	25	750	£1.80
Cauliflower (each)	1.0	100	10	1000	£1.50
Purple sprouting broccoli (kg)	1.0	100	5	500	£2.50
Cabbage (kg)	1.0	100	10	1000	£1.20
Kale (kg)	0.0	100	10	0	£1.50
Broad beans (kg)	1.0	100	5	500	£2.00
Green beans (kg)	1.0	100	5	500	£3.00
Peas (kg)	1.0	100	3	300	£5.00
Sweetcorn (kg)	0.0	100	2	0	£1.50
Courgette (kg)	1.0	100	15	1500	£1.40
Lettuce (mixed / kg)	1.0	100	30	3000	£12.00
Chard (kg)	0.0	100	20	0	£2.00
Potatoes (kg)	1.0	100	52	5200	£1.00
Beetroot (kg)	1.0	100	20	2000	£2.00
Celeriac (kg)	1.0	100	10	1000	£1.20
Parsnip (kg)	1.0	100	15	1500	£0.90
Carrots (kg)	1.0	100	30	3000	£1.30

Total crop value

Total value	Rotation	Area (m²)	Area adjusted by yield*	Standard yields (kg per ha)	Standard yields (kg per m²)
£3,640	Allium	1300.0	975	20000	2
£1,500	Allium	500.0	375	20000	2
£1,350	Allium	625.0	469	12000	1.2
	Total Alliums	**2425.0**	**1818.8**		
£1,500	Brassica	724.6	543	13800	1.38
£1,250	Brassica	1000.0	750	5000	0.5
£1,200	Brassica	500.0	375	20000	2
£0	Brassica	0.0	0	10000	1
	Total Brassicas	**2224.6**	**1668.5**		
£1,000	Legumes	333.3	250	15000	1.5
£1,500	Legumes	1666.7	1250	3000	0.3
£1,500	Legumes	500.0	375	6000	0.6
	Total Legumes	**2500.0**	**1875.0**		
£0	Other	0.0	0	30000	3
£2,100	Other	1500.0	1125	10000	1
£36,000	Other	10000.0	7500	3000	0.3
£0	Other	0.0	0	12000	1.2
	Total Other	**11500.0**	**8625.0**		
£5,200	Potatoes	2080.0	1560	25000	2.5
	Total Potatoes	**2080.0**	**1560.0**		
£4,000	Roots	800.0	600	25000	2.5
£1,200	Roots	500.0	375	20000	2
£1,350	Roots	1000.0	750	15000	1.5
£3,900	Roots	1071.4	804	28000	2.8
	Total Roots	**3371.4**	**2528.6**		
£68,190		Total area of crops	**18075.9**		
		Fertility building / Green manures	**4518.9**		
		Crop failure	**3615.2**		
		Total area of site	**26210.0**		

* high = 75%, medium = 50%, low = 25%

CHAPTER 9

Marketing and selling

So now you've done all the hard work: you've spent a great deal of time finding a plot of suitable land; negotiated a reasonable rent with the landowner, or raised the funds to buy the land; got a business plan and ticked any necessary financial and legal boxes; and, of course, grown your crops and harvested the fruits of your labour! Phew. Now, where are those customers?

It's easy to feel somewhat peeved that customers are not immediately beating down your door, desperate for your luscious veg after all that effort. Although you've thought of little else over the last few months, that doesn't mean that everyone else has – or even that anyone knows about you yet. Word of mouth is a great and powerful tool, but a very slow starter when it comes to marketing: you need to get the message out there as much as possible, and as soon as possible. You'll have had a market in mind before you started growing (or should at least have had a rough idea of who your customers are and what they want) – so now is the time to grab hold of them and blow your own trumpet at them loudly.

Sales routes

Customers fit into two main groups. The first are direct customers – those who are actually going to eat your produce – to whom you may be selling via a market stall, veg van or veg box or bag scheme (including Community Supported Agriculture schemes), or perhaps one large household such as a private country estate. These sales are very desirable, because you can roughly plan ahead for schemes such as veg boxes or what a particular market stall might sell; and if something isn't quite ready in time, you can just box up or take to market what you do have available. It's also a great feeling to be providing food for individuals and families that you get to know, and you can build great relationships with your customers, getting excited about good veg together. The other main (and arguably most important) advantage is that you get a good retail price for your veg – and you get to keep it all, unlike when selling via a shop or other outlet.

However, direct sales can lead to wastage at times, for instance if you pick for a market and don't sell everything, or if customers cancel their boxes at the last minute (it's a good idea to discourage this as much as possible, explaining why, and make sure your cancellation cut-off date each week is before your picking day). Another disadvantage of these kinds of direct sales is that filling lots of individual orders can be fiddly and time-consuming, especially if not done in one go, and requires somewhere to pack and store boxes or orders. If you choose to run a box scheme, you'll also have more administrative duties to fulfil, unless it's kept very small scale and involves people who are really keen on the scheme and are happy to get whatever you have ready that week (so each box identical; no special boxes or dislikes). Many people like the idea of a box scheme, but, unless they are used to regularly preparing a range of fresh produce, can find it a challenge working out what to do with Jerusalem artichokes, asparagus or swedes every week, and so revert to just broccoli and carrots – and if you don't offer that as an option, they may go elsewhere (see Chapter 10 for ideas on keeping your customers).

Indirect customers are those to whom you sell via the wholesale market, through other businesses such as shops and farm shops, cafés, pubs and restaurants, and at events such as weddings or festivals. The advantages of these markets are that they usually send in larger orders, and you can pick the veg when you get the order, so there's no wastage (unless of course you can't sell what's in the field). Many chefs are desperate for high-quality local produce – especially if you can grow more unusual fresh items such as oriental salad leaves or baby coloured carrots – so will be enthusiastic and loyal customers. The orders are often quite reliable too, once you build a solid relationship with the chef or produce manager: it's good to establish a routine of delivering to them perhaps once or twice a week if practical.

Wholesale sales can also be a good way of letting others market your produce for you, such as in shops. It's often good kudos for a shop to have their own pet grower, especially if you grow something special just for them, or if your produce isn't available in any other shop: it's a good story to tell, and most retailers are only too keen to use that story to help sell your produce (and boost the profile of all the other products in the shop at the same time). It also helps them retain customers' loyalty if they can offer something special.

Disadvantages of wholesale sales, however, include the price you get: it's quite common for shops to add up to 100-per-cent mark-up on fresh produce, owing to the short shelf life and risk of wastage, so quite often you'll only be charging as little as half your desired retail price. You will need to check that any wholesale prices still cover your costs and don't leave you out of pocket for that crop (see the crop profitability table in Chapter 8), and that you get the margin that you need in order to keep going. It's tempting to scale down your wholesale price from the price you've seen in a shop for Savoy cabbage, for instance – but sometimes this can leave you out of pocket. It's better, while keeping such a market price in mind, to work out your pricing by how much each crop costs to grow, then add your desired mark-up or profit in order to cover your work (in effect your wages). See page 145 for more about pricing.

You'll also be competing for wholesale business with larger-scale growers, who are likely to be in a position to offer better prices. However, you can push the local and freshness angle – while small-scale growers will not usually be able to compete on price with large growers (although in some cases you'd be surprised), chefs are usually keener than most to get the freshest produce, and many like to support artisan producers.

Another potential problem of wholesale markets is that you can end up being reliant on a few loyal pubs or shops, which will affect your turnover if they close down for a few weeks, have a slow month, or if the management changes.

Because of the pros and cons of each type of market, it's a good idea to hedge your bets and include both direct and indirect customers if possible. So, if you're planning on setting up a market stall or box scheme, then consider pitching to a shop or local pub too, and vice versa – having one or two direct customers who are happy to have whatever is in season is a great way of getting a proper price for a box of veg; plus, if you've sold all your cucumbers to a café, you can include something else in the box without disappointing anyone.

Marketing

Get the word out there! Try to make the most of every opportunity to make sure your local community knows who you are, and what you're selling. Marketing is an exciting part of the business, and can lead to some really creative ways of spreading the message: dreaming up eye-catching leaflets and posters; offering samples and seeing customers' reactions; making a viral ad for online attention – let your imagination run riot!

Leaflets

Whichever market you're growing for, you need to produce some marketing material to promote yourself. Business cards, leaflets and posters are a great and relatively cheap way of telling people about yourself and your market garden, and explaining why your produce is so amazing. Don't tell your life story on your leaflets, however – depending on your set-up and who you're pitching to, just a few lines or bullet points about you, your garden and what you offer should suffice. For door-to-door leaflets, the simpler the design the better, because you'll only have a second or two of a person's attention before they decide to drop it in the recycling. But if you're sending a leaflet to someone who wants some information about what you do, you'll need to put in some more detail, and perhaps make it a bit more personal – a quote from you and anyone else involved can work well. It's a good idea to have a few different leaflets on file, with varying levels of detail and different focus, for attracting different customers. Although these can be easily put together in most desktop publishing programs, it's always worth enlisting someone with design skills to give your material a professional edge. If you know someone in that area, they might be happy to help in return for a veg box; alternatively, professional leaflet companies can be cheaper than you might think.

The main thing people will want to know is why they should buy your veg. Important points to communicate are that your produce is local, therefore very fresh (and so also contributes fewer greenhouse gas emissions from less transport, as well as sequestering carbon via composts and manure in your soil); and, if you grow to organic standards, that it is grown without pesticides or other chemicals (another environmental plus, as well as a healthier option). You could also show that you represent ethical choices: perhaps you're very committed to local jobs at fair wages, and using ethical materials such as recycled equipment and peat-free compost.

You'll have your own unique selling points (USPs), such as convenience if you're delivering free to homes or restaurants, perhaps with no minimum order (though this does mean someone could make you drive miles just for a bunch or two of carrots). Perhaps much of your produce is colour-themed (this could appeal to school or other educational groups: purple carrots, purple cauliflower, purple tomatoes, purple sprouting broccoli . . .). Or maybe you offer voluntary or therapeutic work for disabled or disadvantaged groups. Whatever your USP, don't hide it under a bushel: you're special, so tell people!

It sounds obvious, but do make sure that your leaflet (or preferably leaflets) says clearly and simply what you do – as well as how people can buy your produce. I've seen many leaflets where it's very hard to work out exactly what someone is selling. Include as many contact details as possible: at least a phone number and email address, and your street address with landmarks and perhaps a map if you can sell from the garden gate, market stall or community shop. A website (see page 142) isn't always necessary but could be a bonus.

Overleaf are a couple of my own leaflets, aimed at different audiences. The first is one that I've sent out to farm shops, pubs and restaurants; I've used the second to raise awareness and orders for direct veg boxes at my local football team.

Fitness Veg Box
Only £6

✔ 5 fresh vegetables every week during the summer, full of vitamins, minerals and antioxidants to enhance your fitness programme

✔ Sustainably grown local produce delivered to the training ground

✔ Healthy seasonal food perfect for salads and stir-fries includes: tomatoes; lettuce; cucumber; courgette; mangetout; beans; sweet peppers; carrots; beetroot; spring onions; spinach; radishes

✔ Extra veg, fruit and herbs available, picked the same day

Kate Collyns, Grown Green @ hartley**Farm**
Member of the Wholesome Food Association
Tel: 07957 000000 Email: Kate.Collyns@gmail.com

Social media and websites

Facebook, Twitter, LinkedIn and other social media site contacts are another way for people to get hold of you, or for them to find out more about your garden. Some people love them; some hate them; others see them as a useful tool for business. If you do go down the social media route for marketing, it's important that you understand how to keep your social and business profiles separate – if you want to. If you don't, and you put a picture of yourself after a glass or two of bubbly on Facebook, say, and all your customers are your Facebook Friends, they will be able to see the incriminating pictures too. It's worth remembering . . .

You could set up a separate account in the name of your business: Facebook is useful for those who don't have a website to provide a source of contact details and show pictures (although basic blogs such as Wordpress or Blogger are free to set up and give you more autonomy about how your pages look; they also offer the option to upgrade to a 'proper' website). Twitter is more immediate than Facebook, but also more transient: you can post a short tweet with or without a picture, giving people who choose to follow you an update on what you've been up to – but many people won't see it unless they too are on Twitter at the same time, or they choose to search a theme or look back at your tweets, because the post will get lost in their news feed of other tweets and updates. A combination of social media outlets is useful. Facebook events and Twitter also enable you to find potential customers, and give you a way of contacting them. It's definitely worth giving these media a try at least, and seeing if you can keep it up.

In order to keep online interest on social media, however, you will need to write regular updates: at least once a week, preferably more; and let people know what you have available for sale, and when. Websites tend to be more static, and are usually updated less frequently (some people just use them as a cyber directory to list who they are and what they do), although regularly updated news pages and links to other sites and blogs from your website will encourage more visitors to your site.

There are a number of website hosts available, charging just a few pounds a month; and many also offer easy off-the-peg websites, which can be customised to look more individual. You could also employ a professional web designer to sort you out a site with bells and whistles: expect to pay £500-1000, depending on what you want the website to do (for instance, if you want customers to order bespoke veg boxes and place different vegetables in a virtual veg box, and pay online, you'll have to fork out more).

Advertising

If you're operating on a small scale with limited funds, you probably won't be in a position to advertise very much, or perhaps even at all, but it is worth considering the return from even a small investment – local newspapers, foodie magazines and radio stations can be good sources of direct customers. If you do choose to advertise, make sure you try to get some free editorial space to go with it – or at least ask if this might be possible when negotiating with them: many local listings papers tend to give editorial only to advertisers. Think up some unusual angle on your holding, or simply write a little piece about your launch or other events. This press release should also be sent to all other papers, magazines and radio stations you can think of, whether you're advertising with them or not, because some may find it interesting and have page space they need filling with news stories or events pieces.

At the farm where I did my apprenticeship, we grew melons in a polytunnel, and I'd heard of someone years ago using bras to support melons as they grew. So we sent out a note to our customers, asking for old bras for our huge melons . . . As well as creating a fun talking point with our existing customers (double entendres galore for months), we also sent a press release about it to all the local papers, and one picked up the story and came out to take some pictures. The next day *The Sun*, Radio 2 and others had also picked up on it because they keep an eye on local newspapers, so we got a mountain of free publicity. This was all just before an open day at the farm, and we had a huge turnout. We were also approached a couple of years later by a Japanese television company who wanted to buy the rights to our pictures of melons in bras for a TV advert – so we made a little extra money for the farm for no extra work! It's amazing what a luckily timed press release can do, especially in the 'silly season' for news during the summer, when Parliament is closed and news can be a bit slow.

Pricing

Once you have enough produce ready to sell, you need to work out how much of each crop you'll have available for that week or in the next few days, then put together a price list, or a couple of lists for different types of customer (retail and wholesale). Probably the easiest way to do this is to make a simple spreadsheet with a column for the type of crop (variety information can also be useful and interesting to potential customers), together with what the unit is (i.e. whether the price is per kilo, such as for loose carrots, or for each item, such as an individual lettuce or a bunch of carrots – this could be a separate column if you prefer), a column for the price per unit, and a column for customers to state their required quantity if they are filling in and emailing the form back to you with what they'd like. It's also important to include your contact information on the sheet. These lists will need updating regularly (a new list every week is usual), so you can let customers know what you have, what's sold out, and what's coming up. Overleaf is one of my own price list forms.

Grown Green

Produce available from Monday 10/9/13	Price (each / per kg)	
Vegetables		
Baby beetroot bunch, each	£0.90	
Chilli pepper, green hot, each	£0.25	
Kale bags, Red Russian / Cavolo Nero, each	£1.20	
Leeks, young, per kg	£4.20	
Mini cucumber, each	£0.60	
Rainbow chard, per bag	£0.90	
Rocket, per bag	£1.20	
Tomatoes, mixed heirloom, per 500g punnet	£1.60	
Tomatoes, mixed heirloom, per kg	£3.20	
Salads		
Micro salad leaf mixed punnet: from Green Frills mustard, Red Frills mustard, mizuna, mibuna, leaf celery, fennel, leaf radish; each	£2.60	
Herbs		
Basil / lemon basil, per bag	£1.20	
Garlic chives & flowers, per bag	£1.20	
Lovage, per bag	£1.20	
Sage, per bag	£1.20	
Winter savory, per bag	£1.20	
Total		
Coming soon:		
Dwarf French beans, mixed colour (purple, yellow, green), per bag	£1.25	
Bell peppers, per kilo	£2.50	
Courgettes, per kilo	£2	
Sweetcorn, each	£0.50	
Squash, per kilo	£1.40	
Winter salads (Oriental mix), per bag	£1.20	

Kate Collyns	Hartley Farm, Winsley, Bradford
Tel: 07957 000000	on Avon BA15 2JB
Email: kate.collyns@gmail.com	Free delivery
	No minimum order

Quantity available	Quantity ordered: please enter here	Subtotal	Please send in all orders at least 24 hours before delivery
4	0	£0.00	
10	0	£0.00	
4	0	£0.00	
4	0	£0.00	
4	0	£0.00	
4	0	£0.00	
4	0	£0.00	
6	0	£0.00	
5	0	£0.00	
2	0	£0.00	
2	0	£0.00	
2	0	£0.00	
2	0	£0.00	
2	0	£0.00	
2	0	£0.00	
		£0.00	
4			
4			
15			
40			
20			
20			

Deciding on the price to charge is quite tricky, and can be an art in itself. It's pretty hard trying to base a price on what the crop has cost you to produce, but you can get a rough idea, as described in Chapter 8. The more of a crop you grow and successfully harvest, of course, the cheaper its production cost will be.

You will need to decide what you'd like your profit margin to be. Do you just want to cover your costs, including your own wages – what will you pay yourself? Or do you want or need to add extra profit on top of this, perhaps for any other shareholders in the business? Once you've worked out your rough production costs for each crop, you will then add your profit margin on top. However, keep checking the end figure: even if your profit margin is just 10-20 per cent, you could sometimes end up with a price that is much higher or lower than the average market price. So, for example, potatoes grown on a small scale can have a production cost at least two or three times higher than the market price, without even adding a profit margin, whereas a bag of rocket could be produced for much less than the market price if you grow enough, so your profit margin can be fairly substantial and the end price will still fit into the market. If you find that you won't get the price you need, you will need to think again about the types of crops that you are growing.

It makes sense to do some research to get an idea of pricing: by looking at other wholesalers' price lists, visiting local farm shops and markets, visiting market websites such as DEFRA's (GOV.UK) for their price guides, and also keeping an eye on supermarket prices. However, supermarket prices can often be misleading, since sometimes they will offer 'loss-leaders' on fresh produce: offering a very low price and even losing money on a product, in order to draw customers in who will then buy more expensive items too. So don't set too much store by other retailers' prices if they're not for quite the same niche product as yours, since your customers will often be aware (or you can make them aware) that they may be paying more for your product because it's high quality, local and fresher. At the end of the day, ask yourself whether you'd pay your own asking price for your veg. Above all, do beware of under-pricing, because it's pretty awkward to raise a price quickly once you've started selling a product.

Sample boxes

Once you've got your price list sorted, it's time to start selling. You may have one or two customers lined up already; otherwise, a good way of getting potential customers interested is to offer them a free taster of what you have on offer. You'll already have a good idea of the kind of people and businesses in the area to approach from your market research: so, find a contact number or email address, take a deep breath, and go for it. If emailing a potential wholesale customer, send them a brief line or two about who you are and what you do; attach a relevant leaflet about your business for more information, and a current price list. Suggest that you come to see them and bring a few samples of your current produce for them to try: a range is good if possible, depending on the season – so, something leafy, something rooty, and maybe some herbs and flowers if you're selling them too – whatever looks, smells, feels and tastes best, and will have the most impact.

When you go to meet them or to drop off the samples, take another printed price list with you, and a business card so your contact details are always on hand for them. Many chefs and other buyers will probably be very interested in what you're doing, so be ready to tell them more about your plans, and about the range of crops you're growing for the rest of the year. Don't fret too much if you don't have a huge range at the moment: most will understand the seasonality of produce. As long as you have some things available now, and the promise of others soon, you'll be good to go. Ask them what they're looking for too: don't forget that one of your selling points is that you're a small and flexible set-up, so you can pick to order, and maybe consider growing or picking particular plants that they're looking for and can't get elsewhere (herb flowerheads and smaller delicate leaves are popular with chefs, whereas shops tend to prefer larger veg that keeps well and is easy for customers to peel and prepare).

Similarly, if you're hoping to attract more direct customers at a market or via a box scheme, say, you could try offering people small free samples of really fresh produce to try before they buy – a few spicy salad leaves or halved tomatoes, for example. This often works well, especially for more unusual produce, and provides a good talking point.

Sales growth

While you'll be trying to collect a number of new customers at the beginning of your venture, it probably won't be sustainable for you to continue finding extra sales at the same rate, given the limits of your land area and the amount you can produce. Once you have struck that balance of selling pretty much everything you have, though, that doesn't mean you can rest on your laurels; at any minute customers might change their minds and shop elsewhere, or change job and move; or it might simply be quiet for a week or two (the end of summer is always a great time for veg, yet many people are on holiday, so finding a market for your gluts can be tough). So it's a good idea to have your next target customers in mind, ready to approach, just in case one revenue stream begins to dry up.

You can also find extra customers from every part of your life: local shops and post offices; hobbies and sports activities; school; a visit to the dentist, doctor or hairdresser; neighbours and family friends. Talk to everyone about what you do – many people will be keen to find out more or to try some veg, since it's often hard to find good-quality fresh local produce. Don't forget that what you're doing is brilliant, brave and still uncommon! Food is essential for life, and growing it in a sustainable way is essential for us all in the longer term too.

Marketing and selling checklist

- Establish whether you'll specialise in direct ('retail') or wholesale sales: a combination of the two is best, but it doesn't have to be 50:50. Direct sales means more potential profit and solid customer relationships; wholesale sales are good ways to get rid of gluts, and can move the marketing onus to the shops and restaurants you sell to.

- Think about what your profit margin is going to be – or do you just need to cover your costs? Work out your pricing strategy. Note: it's unlikely you will become a millionaire by selling vegetables from a market garden.

- Start marketing as soon as possible. Use as many outlets as possible: leaflets and posters; websites, social media and weblogs. Will you invest funds in advertising? Consider holding events to raise awareness and create free publicity for your business, such as a launch day, volunteer day or local food festival.

- Send out price lists and leaflets to prospective customers, and make some sample boxes to show wholesale customers, as well as small samples or tasters for direct sales such as at market stalls.

CHAPTER 10

Challenges ahead

Congratulations – you are now running your own market garden business! Selling your first box of produce is so exciting and scary: what will people think of it? Will it change their lives? Will they order some more? The chances are that they will love it – so relax and enjoy the moment.

However, I'm afraid that the slightly sobering news is that the hard work is not over: rather like the crops, the business side of things is a perennial demand too. Some years are especially challenging, environmentally or economically (or both, in the case of rain- and recession-hit 2012). Global warming will only increase the incidence of extreme weather events and patterns;

some customers can be fair-weather friends too, when other demands on their pockets arise; and the attention given to genetically modified food and seeds is also persistently causing a problem for organic growers, since traditional seed varieties aren't being well maintained by the seed companies, and the spread of GM crops could mean unintentional contamination in organic fields. Therefore you'll pretty much always have to remain on your toes, and be as flexible as you possibly can, in order to survive. On the other hand, coming up with solutions to these challenges can make running a market garden so exciting and rewarding – so embrace the uncertainty if you can, and you'll go from strength to strength.

Reliability of production

Consistency is very important in any business; but it can be hard to achieve when you're so dependent on the weather and other external factors such as pests and disease. Ensuring your production stays reliable is essential, so consider the following ideas to help you achieve that.

Crop diversity

A market garden is, to some extent, naturally designed to be resilient to difficult seasons and fluctuating weather patterns, because a range of crops are grown, so something at least should yield well in any given year. However, there are ways to make sure that as many crops as possible do well.

Varieties: some particular varieties are better suited to stresses, droughts and floods than others, so check when you're ordering seed.

Seed saving: saving your own seed is very easy for some crops (e.g. beans, peas, squashes, tomatoes, herbs), and any seed you select will already have a head start and be well suited to your own particular climatic and soil conditions.

Perennials: these take time to establish in the first year or so, but many will keep going for years, with very little maintenance. Consider more perennial herbs, fruit bushes, vegetables such as asparagus, and trees if you have room. An agroforestry system also means that you maximise crop production from three dimensions, rather than just at ground level, as well as providing shelter and wildlife habitat.

Research: consider getting involved in trials and scientific research into more resilient varieties, helping scientists and seed companies produce affordable and useful crops that will eventually also directly benefit you.

Specialising: even if you do choose to specialise in particular crops, it could still be worth trying to include as many different varieties as possible. For instance, if you decide to concentrate on salads, including

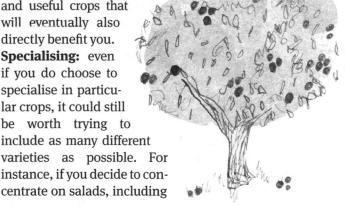

lots of types will keep you covered in case of mishaps – plus mark you out for having such a wide range.

Further diversification

Diversification has been a buzzword in family farms for years, and it's worth keeping in mind if relevant for your business. If possible, it's good to try to make every angle work for you: whether it's allowing campers to stay (or even better, to come and help too!), or offering bed and breakfast, and perhaps holiday-specific festivals, secret supper clubs or a pick-your-own section. Introducing livestock such as chickens is another potential revenue stream, as is starting your own farmers' market or opening up your market garden to charity groups and therapeutic courses. You could also offer courses on vegetable gardening for any local enthusiastic allotmenteers and gardeners, or even start a café or healthy fruit-and-salad van business, delivering snacks to offices.

Protected cropping

In very wet and cold years, protected cropping in polytunnels and greenhouses really does come into its own, and repays any investment; plus it extends the growing season in spring and winter, whatever the weather. In 2012, the only carrots and beetroot I had were rows I drilled in the tunnels out of desperation. If you think you might have room for another polytunnel, or you come across a bargain of a second-hand tunnel, my advice is definitely to put as many tunnels up as you can. They are a hassle to build and clad, or to find spare parts for if missing, but it really will be worth it.

It's also worth making 'back-up' sowings of as many crops as possible too, just in case the first (and second) lot gets eaten or ruined by weather and pests. Little and often is usually best, especially for crops with cheap seed.

Predicting climate change is a tricky business: it may be that we have wetter summers, or drier ones, so try to prepare for every eventuality if possible. More nets will keep more pests off crops; more fleeces will protect against early or late frosts; and more irrigation will keep produce watered in times of drought.

The wider community

You're not alone! It's easy to feel down at times if you work on your own most of the time, and have no one to talk to about growing, the market and weather problems. However, there is strength in numbers: so get involved in meetings and events where possible, to swap stories, come up with new ideas, convert your community and reignite your own enthusiasm for veg.

Local growers' groups

Joining or even setting up a local growers' group is definitely worth it, especially if you're not a very experienced grower. Members meet up several times a year at each other's holdings for a chat and farm walk (some groups are more formal and have a strict agenda), and it's a great way to socialise and swap ideas. Groups can club together and buy things in bulk, such as plants or compost, which reduces the price for everyone. Members can also sell their produce together as a co-operative, or to each other. Above all, it's great to meet up and compare notes on the season and crops, moan about the weather, and get some reassurance that you're doing a good job.

Certification

Although you might want to grow sustainably, you may have already decided that organic certification is not for you when you start out. However, it's worth re-evaluating this regularly: there are many benefits to being certified (contacts, guidance, courses, being able to use logos and the word 'organic'), which may prove more beneficial in the future, especially if you want to develop the business.

On the other hand, you may go for organic certification to start with, but a few years down the line need to reassess your finances and stop paying for certification, especially if you only sell very locally. This is a big step, however, because not only will you not be able to call yourself 'organic' any more, but you'll also have to go through up to two years' conversion again if you change your mind in the future.

Education

One of the best ways that a small-scale market gardener can contribute to the sustainable food movement, as well as promote themselves as a business, is to hold open days and invite people on to the holding. It would be great to see more horticulture, agriculture and food awareness being taught in schools and appearing on television and in other media, but even so, the best way that people can understand what sustainable growing is all about is to experience it for themselves. Soil is still so little valued and understood by most people – yet it's where all food comes from. It is the perfect starting point for people to understand the issues surrounding food production: from intensive 'factory farming' to chemical inputs and genetically modified food. While it can be difficult trying to communicate all the benefits of sustainable local food on a leaflet, if people see what you do, and compare it to big agriculture, realising that what they might think of as growing and farming now exists on only a small scale, then your job is done for you. Who would choose unsustainable food once they understand what's involved?

So have an open-gate policy as much as possible, and encourage individual customers, chefs and shopkeepers to come and visit. As well as spreading the word, they can see exactly what you're growing, and plan their menus and stock lists around your forthcoming produce!

Staying solvent

With all the other million-and-one things going on in
your head, a year can slip by and you may not know
how the business is really doing if you're not on top of
your paperwork. As noted in Chapter 6, little-and-
often accounting is the best way of tackling things like
invoices and expenses, and prevents the paperwork
stacking up. It also helps you get a feel for how the
business is doing, other than simply looking at your
bank balance or order numbers. It's really important
to keep on top of payments: although an invoice might
have been sent out to the customer just after you
delivered your produce, it's easy for them to forget to
pay, and if you don't send out reminders, some people
simply won't pay at all (and not always because
they've forgotten). Late and missing payments are the
bane of small businesses, which is another reason
why cash on delivery, or a cash-only market stall, is so
attractive. Try to include chasing up missing payments as part of your monthly routine, and your cash
flow will look a lot healthier as a result. Tell long-
standing debtors that you'll put their orders on hold
until they've cleared their debts, and have a cut-off
limit in mind when checking how much anyone owes
you. Keeping a regular eye on this will at least stop
any con-men making off with thousands as the unpaid
orders rack up, even if they manage to swindle a small
amount from you. The small claims court or debt
retrieval companies can be a last resort for systematic
bad debtors, but can often end up costing you time
and even more money.

It's worth keeping track of roughly what each crop has cost and made each year (see Chapter 8), to see if it makes sense to ditch some that may be losing you money consistently. Don't beat yourself up for the first year or so, though, or give up within 12 months if you're not earning any money. Generally, small businesses will make a loss for the first year (owing to start-up costs), then hopefully break even or even make a small profit for some wages for the second year, and from then on you should be making a profit (or the business will be paying for itself and sustainable, if profit isn't the plan). If you expect to become rich, you will probably be disappointed, but if you want to just earn some extra money, make a living or even make enough to give other people jobs, you should certainly be able to achieve that.

Customer loyalty

This doesn't seem to be valued so much these days, and it's not just large corporations that are the culprits – indeed, big companies often recognise the importance and psychology of good customer service. It's often smaller businesses that have incredibly bad or incompetent customer service – some seem to resent selling you anything at all. Make sure you don't become one of these people: it's unlikely that you'll have a captive market, so people will just go elsewhere.

Making the initial sale isn't the end of the selling and marketing job: in order to keep customers, you'll have to be consistent, reliable, and sell them great-quality produce. While it's not the end of the world if you can't fulfil an order one week because of a lack of rain or a pest attack for example, it's good to let customers know as soon as possible that they can't have what they've ordered, so they can make alternative arrangements. It's worth (briefly) explaining the reasons why too, to keep them in touch with the market garden and feel involved in the process – and to demonstrate why you've had to withdraw the crop. Most customers will understand and sympathise if you have a pest or weather problem, but do try to anticipate potential problems as far as possible. For instance, if you're unsure whether you'll have enough of something the following week, don't include it on the price list, or don't include it on every list. You can always let customers know nearer the picking day whether something is now available – which will be a positive change, rather than taking it away if it's not ready and thereby creating a negative impression.

Invite customers to follow you on your social media streams (if you're going down that route), produce regular newsletters and recipe ideas for their veggies, and chat to them about what you're up to as much as possible. Open days, volunteer days and other events are also a good way of making sure customers feel that they are part of your exclusive club, and that they are valued.

Keep an eye on what other veg your wholesale customers are selling or cooking, and remind them of your produce if they shop elsewhere. Many chefs will want to know what you've got coming up in the next month, so they can plan menus, and shops will want certain things at certain times (such as salad bags on Bank Holidays and at sunny weekends for barbecues), so keep these in mind when working out your sowing and planting schedule.

Ask your customers before your season gets going whether there's anything else they'd like you to grow: consider sending a questionnaire out in winter, or producing one for market or shop customers. You don't have to go along with every suggestion of course, or act on every single bit of feedback, but it's interesting if the same suggestion appears on a number of replies. Asking for feedback is, again, a good way of reinforcing the link between you and your customers. Our wider consumerist society can often leave us feeling powerless, so if people feel as though they have real input into something, that can only be a good thing – and they'll come back for more.

Above all, try to take stock every now and then, and enjoy what you're doing. Take a break on a sunny June day to lie back in the warm grass and listen to the bees buzzing around the flowers, watch tadpoles wiggling in a wildlife pond or blackbirds frolicking among the beans, and remember why you wanted to start a market garden in the first place. You are producing healthy, fresh food for yourself, family, friends and community, and you're also doing your bit to look after the land and wildlife for future generations to enjoy. Good work!

Meeting challenges checklist

- Look at ways to continue producing your crops as consistently as possible. If you're worried that your favourite varieties of seeds may disappear in the future, try saving your own seed. Try a range of varieties too, in case one specific variety fails that year. Try out some perennials: once established they'll have a strong root base to better cope with fluctuating weather.

- Prepare for more extreme weather as much as possible: keep a lookout for useful tools and equipment such as irrigation systems, good-quality fine-mesh nets and more polytunnels.

- Think about ways to diversify, to be more resilient in the future. Will keeping animals on the holding, for example, save or make you money in the long run? Could holidaymakers pay to stay and work on your farm?

- Get involved with the local growers' community, as well as the communities of your local villages, cities and towns. Throw your gates open to the public when practical, or club together with other growers or local businesses and arrange local food festivals and events. Continue to keep in mind whether organic certification is right for you, and whether the many benefits outweigh the costs.

- Keep a sharp eye on your accounts, and work out whether you can save money in any particular area. Pay particular attention to outstanding debts from customers, and chase any unpaid bills.

- Remember why you wanted to start a market garden in the first place: you are a real wealth-maker, can produce food for your local community, and enjoy nature and the great outdoors while you're doing it. Give your friends in a cramped and dark office a cheery wave on a summer's day as you go past with your sunglasses on and arms full of fresh healthy produce.

Growing and business calendar

Here is an example of my basic annual calendar for growing ten popular profitable crops: salads, including lettuce; leeks; herbs; tomatoes; carrots; chard; brassicas; beetroot; courgettes and cucumbers. Weeding will also need to be fitted in regularly, but will depend on your soil, weed burden, site and weather. I have also included the most important business dates to remember – and some useful sales dates to keep in mind. Any rent or other bill deadlines will of course depend on your set-up – but the end of the tax year is applicable to everyone, and, if you have registered for VAT, you will need to send in a quarterly VAT return (your first due date will depend on when you registered).

January
† NB Many kitchens shut down in the New Year for their holidays
- Fill in VAT return
- Pay rent
- Pay business insurance
- Service any machinery
* Tax return deadline

February

- Maintain compost heap, fencing and polytunnels (e.g. patch up holes, mend doors)
- Visit other growers' holdings and attend local growers' meetings
- Sow tomatoes indoors with heat
- Sow lettuce in modules (several varieties), then every two to three weeks until autumn

March

† NB Easter (March/April) is a busy time for shops and restaurants, but many people cancel veg box deliveries while away
- Drill leeks
- First ground cultivation
- Sow brassicas (kale, broccoli, cabbage)
- Pot on tomatoes and feed if necessary

April

† End/start of tax year
■ Fill in VAT return
- Second ground cultivation
- Drill beetroot and chard
- Drill carrots
- Plant out lettuce (fleece if necessary) and any brassica crops if ready (net these against pigeons)
- Plant tomatoes with support, string or netting
- Sow early courgettes
- Sow cucumbers
- Sow or drill herbs, and again every few weeks for fast-growing annuals (coriander, flat parsley, basil)
- Start hoeing and hand-weeding drilled and planted crops, then every few weeks over the summer

May

- Sow green manure on ley part of rotation, and undersow suitable crops such as courgettes
- Drill more beetroot for bunching
- Plant out courgettes (cover with fleece if still cool, but check regularly for slugs)
- Plant cucumbers with support, string or nettings
- Plant out herbs
- Plant brassicas; net against pigeons
- Net carrots against carrot root fly; check for slugs regularly

June

- Third ground cultivation
- Estimate harvest dates for crops and begin marketing, leafleting and advertising
- Plant out leeks; net against leek moth
- Side-shoot indeterminate tomatoes (not bush varieties) every week or two to encourage tall growth up supports
- Begin harvesting early courgettes, then check every two or three days
- Begin harvesting herbs (only lightly for perennials)

July

- † NB school holidays start, many people away (good for tourist destinations)
- ■ Fill in VAT return
- Drop off sample boxes to prospective wholesale customers
- Begin harvesting tomatoes, then every two to three days
- Begin harvesting cucumbers, then every one or two days
- Begin harvesting baby carrots for bunching
- Begin harvesting beetroot and chard
- Begin harvesting summer brassicas

August

- Sow first batch of winter salads, then every two or three weeks until October
- Begin harvesting any ready baby leeks

September

- † NB school holidays end; September is a good time to hold an open day or a volunteer day
- Pinch out top shoots of tomatoes, stop watering them (unless extremely dry) and begin to de-leaf plants if blight threatens
- Top/mow green manures

October

- Fill in VAT return
- Plant out winter salads in polytunnel when ready
- Harvest any pumpkins and store in a warm dry place ready for Hallowe'en
- Harvest maincrop beetroot and carrots and store in a cool dry place for use

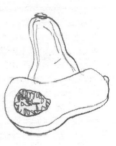

November

- When tomatoes stop producing, compost stems and plant more salads
- Fleece any remaining crops if a hard frost threatens

December

- † Prepare for Christmas craziness: especially popular are potatoes, Brussels sprouts, red cabbage, parsnips, carrots, swedes, salads and herbs
- Spread composts for spring if using no-dig methods

Resources

This directory* is not exhaustive, but provides good starting points for all the areas that you will need to consider when setting up your market garden.

General

Community Supported Agriculture (CSA) Network
www.communitysupportedagriculture.org.uk
Resources and advice.

Federation of Small Businesses
Tel: 0808 202 0888
www.fsb.org.uk
Advice available for members on a range of issues.

National Farmers' Union (NFU)
Tel: 024 7685 8500
www.nfuonline.com
Membership of over 55,000 farmers and growers; get your voice heard and keep abreast of national campaigns.

Organic Growers Alliance
www.organicgrowersalliance.co.uk
Membership and campaigning group offering advice and events information.

Soil Association
Tel: 0117 314 5000
www.soilassociation.org
Campaigning charity and certifying organisation; also holds training events.

*Available as a pdf with live hyperlinks at www.greenbooks.co.uk/gfp-live-links

World Wide Opportunities on Organic Farms (WWOOF)
www.wwoof.org.uk
Membership charity teaching organic principles, and source of willing and often experienced volunteers.

Chapter 2
Finding land

Land

Church of England
www.churchofengland.org/about-us/structure/
churchlawlegis/property.aspx
Landowner: use the postcode finder on the website to find your nearest church.

Ecological Land Co-operative (ELC)
Tel: 07963 955338
http://ecologicalland.coop
Affordable opportunities for ecological land-based businesses.

The Land Workers' Alliance
http://landworkersalliance.org.uk
UK branch of La Via Campesina, the International Peasant's Movement, representing small-scale producers of food, fibres and fuel.

The National Allotment Society
Tel: 01536 266576
www.nsalg.org.uk
Resources and advice.

National Farmers' Union (NFU)
See page 170

National Trust Lettings
www.nationaltrust.org.uk/article-1356401668163/
Landowner offering farm tenancies.

Organic Growers Alliance
See page 170

Reclaim the Fields
www.reclaimthefields.org
Campaigns for access to land.

Soil Association Land Trust
Tel: 0117 987 4601
www.soilassociation.org/landtrust
Branch of the Soil Association administering land held in trust available for organic projects.

UK Land Directory
www.uklanddirectory.org.uk
Land and land agents' online directory.

UK Land & Farms
Tel: 01264 334747
www.uklandandfarms.co.uk
Website specialising in sales and rentals of farms and smallholdings, run by the Agricultural Mortgage Corporation plc.

World Wide Opportunities on Organic Farms (WWOOF)
See page 171

Soil

Environment Agency: Find a soil testing laboratory
www.environment-agency.gov.uk/business/regulation/31835.aspx

Laverstoke Park Farm: Soil laboratory services
Tel: 01256 772667
www.laverstokepark.co.uk/soil_testing_laboratory.aspx
Soil analysis and testing.

NRM Laboratories: Horticulture and fresh produce tests
Tel: 01344 886338
www.nrm.uk.com/services.php?service=horticulture
A range of analysis services, including soil analysis and testing.

Community

Community Supported Agriculture (CSA) Network
See page 170

Growzones
www.growzones.com
Community project: advice on setting up community growing groups.

Transition Towns Network
www.transitionnetwork.org
Global network of community projects to build local resilience.

Chapter 3
Finding a market

Local Foods
www.localfoods.org.uk
Local food directory.

National Farmers' Retail & Markets Association
(FARMA)
Tel: 0845 458 8420
www.farma.org.uk
Farmers' markets organisers.

National Market Traders Federation
Tel: 01226 749021
www.nmtf.co.uk
Find a local market.

Startups: Market stalls
www.startups.co.uk/market-stall_3.html
Advice on starting a market stall.

Chapter 4
Essential equipment

Tools

BHGS
Tel: 01386 444100
www.bhgsltd.co.uk
Wide range of growing equipment and supplies, including packaging.

Blackberry Lane
Tel: 07792 592068
www.blackberrylane.co.uk
Supplier of market garden tools, including EarthWay seeders.

Freecycle
www.freecycle.org
Local networks for recycling unwanted goods, including equipment.

Hawken Knives
Tel: 07790 626952
www.hawken-knives.co.uk
Bespoke handmade growers' knives and other tools.

LBS Horticultural Supplies
Tel: 01282 873333
www.lbsbuyersguide.co.uk/home-trade
Wide range of growing equipment and supplies.

The Market Gardener
Tel: 07952 573584
www.themarketgardener.co.uk
Supplier of Terradonis Seeders.

PG Horticulture
Tel: 01327 828373
www.pghorticulture.co.uk
Wide range of growing equipment and supplies.

Wolf Garten
Tel: 0845 270 7603
www.wolfgarten-tools.co.uk
Wide range of hand tools.

Wondermesh
Tel: 01561 377946
www.wondermesh.co.uk
New and second-hand insect netting and Enviromesh.

Polytunnels

Clovis Lande
Tel: 01622 873900
www.clovis.co.uk
Manufactures and sells tunnels and accessories.

First Tunnels
Tel: 01282 601253
www.firsttunnels.co.uk
Manufactures and sells tunnels and accessories.

Northern Polytunnels
Tel: 01282 873120
www.northernpolytunnels.co.uk
Manufactures and sells tunnels and accessories.

Buying and erecting second hand single span polytunnels,
Sam Blenkharn
www.organicgrowersalliance.co.uk/node/1134
Thorough free guide to constructing polytunnels.

The Polytunnel Handbook, Andy McKee and Mark Gatter
Green Books, 2008
A starting point for putting up smaller tunnels.

How to Grow Food in Your Polytunnel: All year round,
Mark Gatter and Andy McKee
Green Books, 2010
How to make the most of your polytunnel space.

Seeds

CN Seeds
Tel: 01353 699413
www.cnseeds.co.uk
Micro green seeds, vegetables and flowers.

Moles Seeds
Tel: 01206 213213
www.molesseeds.co.uk
*Wide range of conventional flower and vegetable seeds;
some organic.*

The Real Seed Catalogue
Tel: 01239 821107
www.realseeds.co.uk
Heritage seeds.

Stormy Hall Seeds
Tel: 01287 661368
www.stormy-hall-seeds.co.uk
Biodynamic seeds.

Tamar Organics
Tel: 01579 371182
www.tamarorganicspro.co.uk
Organic vegetable and flower seeds.

Tuckers Seeds
Tel: 01364 652233
www.tuckers-seeds.com
Conventional and organic seeds.

Transplants and seedlings

Delflands Nurseries
Tel: 01354 740553
www.delfland.co.uk
Suppliers of a wide range of seedling transplants.

Walcot Organic Nursery
Tel: 01905 841587
www.walcotnursery.co.uk
Fruit trees and soft fruit plants available.

Welsh Fruit Stocks
Tel: 01497 851209
www.welshfruitstocks.co.uk
Suppliers of soft fruit plants.

Wessex Plants
Tel: 01934 876435
www.wessexplants.co.uk
Propagates a wide range of transplants.

Compost suppliers

Carbon Gold
Tel: 0117 244 0032
www.carbongold.com
Made with biochar and coir.

Fertile Fibre
Tel: 01432 853111
www.fertilefibre.com
Made with coir.

West Riding Organics
Tel: 01706 379944
www.westridingorganics.co.uk
Reclaimed peat.

Chapter 5
Raising the money

Loans

The Co-operative Bank
Tel: 0844 844 8844
www.co-operativebank.co.uk
*Free banking for FSB (Federation of Small Businesses)
members.*

Government Funding
www.governmentfunding.org.uk
*Funding information for voluntary and other organisations
available to subscribers.*

The Start Up Loans Company
www.startuploans.co.uk
Government-backed business for 18-30-year-olds.

Sustainable Investing
www.sustainableinvesting.net
Online community for sustainable investors.

Triodos Bank
Tel: 0800 328 2181
www.triodos.co.uk
Ethical lender.

UK Sustainable Investment and Finance Association
http://uksif.org
Find an ethical financial adviser.

Crowdfunding

Buzzbnk
www.buzzbnk.org
Crowdfunder specialising in ethical ideas.

Kickstarter
www.kickstarter.com
The world's largest funding platform for creative projects, using peer-to-peer investment.

Charities and trusts

The Ashden Trust
Tel: 020 7410 0330
www.ashdentrust.org.uk
Offers grants programmes focusing on climate change and sustainable development.

Heinz Charitable Trust
www.heinz.co.uk/ourcompany/sustainability/
economicsustainability
Promotes the quality of life in communities.

The Kindling Trust
Tel: 0161 226 2242
www.kindling.org.uk
Support for ecological projects in the north-west.

Perennial: Gardeners' Royal Benevolent Society
www.perennial.org.uk/helping_you/bursaries.aspx
Lironi training fund available.

Prince's Trust
Tel: 0800 842842
www.princes-trust.org.uk
Low-rate loans and grants for growers available through the Kanabus Fund. (Contact your regional office to find out more.)

Sainsbury Family Charitable Trusts
Tel: 020 7410 0330
www.sfct.org.uk
Hub for a number of Sainsbury Family trusts.

Training and other funding

Grants for Horticulturists
www.grantsforhorticulturists.org.uk
Portal linking to possible grant sources.

Heritage Horticulture Skills Scheme (HHSS)
www.hhss.co.uk/en_gb/home
Provides traineeships in heritage horticultural period techniques.

Lantra Awards
Tel: 024 7669 6996
www.lantra-awards.co.uk
Offers a range of training programmes.

Making Local Food Work
Tel: 01993 810730
www.makinglocalfoodwork.co.uk
Based at the Plunkett Foundation, which can also offer other training opportunities.

Natural England: Environmental Stewardship Scheme
Tel: 0300 060 0011
www.naturalengland.gov.uk/ourwork/farming/funding/
es/default.aspx
*How to apply for the Entry Level Stewardship and
Organic Entry Level Stewardship funds.*

Skills Funding Agency
http://skillsfundingagency.bis.gov.uk/training
*Discretionary Learner Support and other programmes
can help with training costs.*

Wales Council for Voluntary Action
www.sustainablefundingcymru.org.uk
*The latest news on funding and training opportunities in
Wales.*

Business plans

Prince's Trust
See page 180

GOV.UK: Business plans
www.gov.uk/write-business-plan
*Templates to download and advice on completing your
plan.*

Chapter 6
Paperwork Part 1: finance

Business structures

Charity Commission
www.charitycommission.gov.uk
*Resources and advice, including details of who needs to
register as a charitable incorporated organisation (CIO).*

Co-operatives UK
www.uk.coop/start-co-op
Resources and advice for co-operatives, including start-ups.

Community Interest Companies (CIC) Regulator
Tel: 029 2034 6228
www.bis.gov.uk/cicregulator
Information on who can start a CIC.

Companies House
www.companieshouse.gov.uk
Register incorporated companies and check for business names.

Advice and help

Federation of Small Businesses (FSB)
See page 170

GOV.UK: Businesses and self-employed
www.gov.uk/browse/business
Advice on starting up and running a business.

HM Revenue & Customs (HMRC)
Tel (Self Assessment Helpline): 0845 900 0444
www.hmrc.gov.uk
Register for Self Assessment, VAT, PAYE, etc.

HM Revenue & Customs (HMRC) VAT directory
and helpline
Tel: 0300 200 3700
http://tinyurl.com/VATDirectory-food
*This web link shows which food products are zero-rated
for VAT.*

Software and tools

Bucky Box
www.buckybox.com
Veg box software.

CSAware
www.csaware.com
Offers software and help useful particularly for CSAs, including logistics.

PayPal Card Reader
www.paypal.com/uk/webapps/mpp/credit-card-reader
PayPal Here™ lets you accept card payment via your mobile phone.

Streamline
Tel: 0800 010166
www.streamline.com
Credit card processor and terminal provider specialising in small- and medium-sized businesses.

Chapter 7
Paperwork Part 2: law and orders

Contracts and legislation

The British Association for Shooting and Conservation
Tel: 01244 573000
www.basc.org.uk
Detailed advice on pest control and hunting safety.

Citizens Advice Bureau
Tel (England): 08444 111444
Tel (Wales): 08444 772020
www.citizensadvice.org.uk
Find your local office for legal and financial advice.

Department for Environment, Food & Rural Affairs
(DEFRA): Agricultural tenancies
Tel (Innovation and Better Regulation for Farmers
Division): 020 7238 6026
http://archive.defra.gov.uk/foodfarm/farmmanage/
tenancies
Advice on agricultural tenancies and contracts.

Food Standards Agency
Tel: 020 7276 8829
www.food.gov.uk
For the latest news on food policy and standards.

GOV.UK: Legal aid
www.gov.uk/check-legal-aid
Find out whether you are eligible for legal aid.

GOV.UK: Planning permission for farms
www.gov.uk/planning-permissions-for-farms/when-
you-need-it

Health and Safety Executive
www.hse.gov.uk
Offers guidance for employers.

Legislation.gov.uk: Trade Descriptions Act 1968
www.legislation.gov.uk/ukpga/1968/29
The Act in full.

Net Lawman
www.netlawman.co.uk
Downloadable legal contract packages available.

Planning Portal
www.planningportal.gov.uk
*The government's Planning and Building Regulations
resource.*

Sustainweb
www.sustainweb.org/localactiononfood/rules_and_regs
Useful summary of food trading regulations.

Trading Standards Institute
www.tradingstandards.gov.uk
Offers training and advice to ensure your business is compliant with consumer law.

Insurance

NFU Mutual
Tel: 0800 316 4661
www.nfumutual.co.uk
Insurance and other financial services.

Towergate Insurance
Tel: 01482 330300
www.towergateallseasonsinsurance.co.uk
Towergate Allseasons is a specialist horticultural insurer.

Certification

Biodynamic Association
Tel: 01453 759501
www.biodynamic.org.uk
Organic and Demeter (Biodynamic) certification body.

Organic Farmers & Growers (OF&G)
Tel: 01939 291800
www.organicfarmers.org.uk/about-ofg/certification-types/of-g-certification-programme
Organic certification body.

Soil Association Certification
Tel: 0117 914 2406
www.sacert.org
Organic certification body.

Wholesome Food Association
www.wholesome-food.org
Informal membership association used by some growers instead of certifying organic.

Employees

GOV.UK: Holiday entitlement guide
www.gov.uk/holiday-entitlement-rights/entitlement

GOV.UK: Workplace pensions guide
www.gov.uk/workplace-pensions/about-workplace-pensions

HMRC: Guide to holiday, sick and maternity pay
www.hmrc.gov.uk/manuals/esmmanual/esm0544.htm

HMRC: National Insurance guide and calculator
www.hmrc.gov.uk/paye/intro/ni-basics.htm
www.hmrc.gov.uk/calcs/nice.htm

Soil Association Future Growers Scheme
Tel: 0117 987 4601
www.soilassociation.org/futuregrowers
Take on an apprentice or trainee to pass on your skills.

World Wide Opportunities on Organic Farms (WWOOF)
See page 171

Chapter 8
What to grow

Soil Association: CSA horticultural cropping tool
www.soilassociation.org/communitysupportedagriculture/resources/agricultureandlivestock
Free spreadsheet to work out how much of each crop you need.

Chapter 9
Marketing and selling

Marketing tools

Blogger
www.blogger.com
Free blog provider.

Eco Web Hosting
http://ecowebhosting.co.uk
Ethical carbon-neutral web host company.

Vistaprint
Tel: 0800 496 0350
www.vistaprint.co.uk
Economical online printers for business cards, websites and other marketing products.

Wordpress
http://wordpress.com
Free blog provider.

Pricing

GOV.UK: Wholesale fruit and vegetable prices
www.gov.uk/government/publications/wholesale-fruit-and-vegetable-prices
Weekly and monthly national data available.

Soil Association: Horticulture market data
www.soilassociation.org/farmersgrowers/market/marketdata/horticulture
Monthly updates on produce prices.

Chapter 10
Challenges ahead

Research and trials

Duchy Originals Future Farming Programme
www.soilassociation.org/innovativefarming/duchy
originalsfuturefarmingprogramme/abouttheprogramme/
fieldlabs
*Includes field labs, in which growers can take part on
their holdings.*

The Organic Research Centre (ORC)
Tel: 01488 658298
www.organicresearchcentre.com
*Hub of organic-focused research, based at Elm Farm;
also publications and advice.*

Diversification

Organic Holidays
Tel: 01943 870791
www.organicholidays.co.uk
Hub for sustainable breaks and holidays.

Royal Agricultural University
www.rau.ac.uk/business-services
*Holds short training and networking events in Cirencester
for businesses looking to diversify and expand.*

Scotland's Rural College (SRUC)
www.sruc.ac.uk/info/120182/diversification
*Free factsheets on how to diversify into other land-based
areas.*

Further reading

The Fruit Tree Handbook
Ben Pike
Green Books, 2011
Detailed practical guide for growing in the UK.

Grow Your Own Veg
Carol Klein / Royal Horticultural Society
Mitchell Beazley, 2007
Comprehensive guide to growing popular crops.

*How to Grow Perennial Vegetables: Low-maintenance,
low-impact vegetable gardening*
Martin Crawford
Green Books, 2012
Some more unusual ideas for diversification.

New Book of Herbs
Jekka McVicar
Dorling Kindersley, 2004
*Detailed guidance and advice on growing hundreds of
herbs.*

Organic Gardening: The natural no-dig way
Charles Dowding
Green Books, 2013 (colour edition)
*Good all-round guide for veg growers, specialising in
no-tillage methods of production.*

*Salad Leaves for All Seasons: Organic growing from pot
to plot*
Charles Dowding
Green Books, 2008
*Many suggestions for growing valuable salads all year
round.*

Index

Also by Green Books

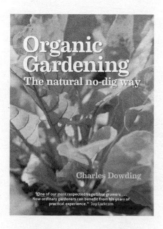

Organic Gardening: The natural no-dig way
Charles Dowding

"Charles is a passionate and accomplished gardener, who grows vegetables of amazing flavour." **Raymond Blanc**

ISBN: 9780857840899
240 pages

How to Grow Winter Vegetables
Charles Dowding

"Charles's book is a paean to our weather, climate and soil. It celebrates all that is good about growing year round, and I guarantee that you'll actually look forward to winter after this read."
Alys Fowler

ISBN: 9781900322881
232 pages

How to Grow Perennial Vegetables: Low-maintenance, low-impact vegetable gardening
Martin Crawford

"This lovely book makes it clear that we are not just missing a trick, we are missing a feast."
Hugh Fearnley-Whittingstall

ISBN: 9781900322843
224 pages

The Fruit Tree Handbook
Ben Pike

"A really well organised, approachable yet thorough guide to sourcing, planting and caring for fruit trees. It's a must for anyone considering anything from a couple of trees to an orchard."
Mark Diacono, River Cottage Head Gardener

ISBN: 9781900322744
352 pages

The Polytunnel Handbook
Andy McKee & Mark Gatter

"A comprehensive guide such as this is long overdue." **Simon McEwan, Editor, *Country Smallholding***

ISBN: 9781900322454
128 pages

How to Grow Food in Your Polytunnel: All year round
Mark Gatter & Andy McKee

"This beautifully presented book covers every possible aspect of polytunnel growing." **Benedict Vanheems, Editor, *Grow it!***

ISBN: 9781900322720
192 pages

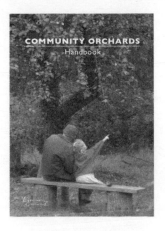

Community Orchards Handbook
Sue Clifford & Angela King

". . . an indispensable and inspiring reference for anyone wanting to enrich the meaning of where they live and introduce biodiversity and delight into their locality." **Kevin McCloud**

ISBN: 9781900322928
232 pages

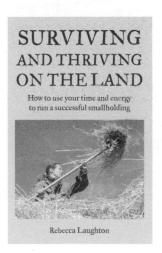

Surviving and Thriving on the Land: How to use your spare time and energy to run a successful smallholding
Rebecca Laughton

"An invaluable and inspiring guide to anyone who seeks to return to their hard-working roots. . . . Henry Thoreau would have been proud of the analysis." **James Crowden, author of *Ciderland* and *In Time of Flood***

ISBN: 9781900322287
328 pages

Allotment Gardening: An organic guide for beginners
Susan Berger

"Essential reading if you've just acquired your own green patch." *Saturday Express*

ISBN: 9781903998540
144 pages

Salad Leaves for All Seasons: Organic Gardening from pot to plot
Charles Dowding

"This is the number one book for anyone who loves salads." **Anna Pavord**

ISBN: 9781900322201
224 pages

Creating a Forest Garden: Working with nature to grow edible crops
Martin Crawford

"This is a seminal piece of work on truly sustainable gardening, written with great spirit and soul." **Alys Fowler**

ISBN: 9781900322621
384 pages

Hot Beds: How to grow early crops using an age-old technique
Jack First

"Jack is a fount of knowledge and the expert on hot beds. When I saw how advanced and healthy his crops were, it proved to me that these ancient old systems still work a treat." **Joe Swift, garden designer and TV presenter**

ISBN: 9780857841063
128 pages

About Green Books

Join our mailing list:
Find out about forthcoming titles, new editions, special offers, reviews, author appearances, events, interviews, podcasts, etc.
www.greenbooks.co.uk/subscribe

How to order:
Get details of stockists and online bookstores. (Remember that you can also order direct from our website.) If you are a bookstore, find out about our distributors or contact us to discuss your particular requirements.
www.greenbooks.co.uk/order

Send us a book proposal:
If you want to write – even if you have just the kernel of an idea – we'd love to hear from you. We pride ourselves on supporting our authors and making the process of book-writing as satisfying and as easy as possible.
www.greenbooks.co.uk/for-authors